Stevee, Lot Bell Pond Books 10/17/95

It's Not My Fault

It's Not My Fault

Tales of a Vermont Doctor

Beach Conger, M.D.

Fulcrum Publishing
Golden, Colorado

To Charlie Davidson and Ron Arky.
It's not their fault either.

Copyright © 1995 Beach Conger

Cover design by Alyssa Pumphrey

Library of Congress Cataloging-in-Publication Data
Conger, Beach
    It's not my fault: tales of a Vermont doctor / Beach Conger.
        p.   cm.
    ISBN 1-55591-223-0 (hc : alk. paper)
    1. Conger, Beach, 1941- . 2. Physicians—Vermont—Biography.
I. Title.
    R154.C554A3   1995
    610'.92—dc20
    [B]   95-32392
                                            CIP

Printed in the United States of America

0 9 8 7 6 5 4 3 2 1

Fulcrum Publishing
350 Indiana Street, Suite 350
Golden, Colorado 80401-5093
800/992-2908

Contents

Prologue

It is not an uncommon experience, when people discover that I have written a book, for them to ask me, "What's it about?" The motive for such inquiry varies. Some, unfortunately the minority, are contemplating reading it. Others are seeking to enlarge their store of conversational wares on the possibility, however remote, that my work might at some future gathering, be a topic for discussion. The vast majority are asking, not with any particular end in mind, but in the simple expectation that the having done so would move the conversational ball from their court to mine.

Regardless of intent, the commodity the questioner expects is the same. A few words, a sentence—two at most—that can be popped into one's department of fast facts, filed under title of books, subtitle friend/doctor written by, from where it can be easily recalled or, should the need not arise, just as easily forgotten.

The question is, to the asker, no big deal, and she could just as easily, and with equal interest, ask my preference in breakfast cereals. To an author it is an entirely different horse. For him, this lightly offered interrogatory would be akin to someone coming up to you out of the cold blue and saying, "And precisely what, Ms. Jones, would you say your life has been all about?" Especially in my case, as my life plays a major role in the drama.

So I want to lay this aboutness issue to rest at the outset. My attempt in this tale, which is a continuing chronicle of my experiences in the town of Dumster, Vermont, will be to convey to the reader the Truth (I use the capital here not to imply that the story is allegorical—it is not—but to emphasize the respect I have for this all but forgotten literary commodity.) of the matters related herein—focusing on that particular aspect of Truth that covers the practice of medicine.

Since I am writing on the basis of events that, if they have not actually happened, at least could, and most certainly should have, Truth will usually be apparent from the tale itself. Sometimes, however, clarification may be necessary. Keeping in mind that discriminating readers do not want to waste their time wading through pages of philosophical gobbledegook, I promise to keep these digressions short and to the point.

One final word. There will be some who, in the course of reading this work, will complain about the *fact* of a particular matter, alleging that it is somewhat to the left or right of the mark and therefore in need of correction. To these people I simply say this. Unfortunate soul that you are, you are in the minority. The sooner you learn what the rest of us have always known, that the greatness of Truth is that it transcends the lowly fact, the better off you will be.

Chapter 1

Bjorøya

Something roused me. The clock showed two A.M. It was too early. Expecting to resume my sleep, I closed my eyes and lay down. I was too late. Dawn had breached my slumber fortifications. I was awake.

Next to me, Trine slept soundly. Tightly cocooned in her *dyne*, she was impervious to anything short of the apocalypse. I slipped out of bed and, in the pale not-quite light, picked my way down the steep staircase of the three-hundred-year-old farmhouse that was the Bech family summer home.

The stairs emptied into a large room. Hanging over one of the chairs were my clothes, still damp from yesterday's rain. Quickly I dressed.

Energized by the reaction between warm skin and cold cloth, I lit the stove, put water to boil, and made my way to a long table that ran almost the length of the room. Heaps of paper—yellow lined legal, perforated computer, envelopes, napkins, and unidentifiable assorted scraps—were scattered in disarray on its surface.

Picking up a cup from the top of one of the piles, I sipped the cold tea of yesterday's labors and sat down to face what, having begun as a big adventure, had now become my nightmare.

Kindly old Doc Conger, once beloved physician of Dumster, what had torn me away from my ministrations to the sick and brought me to this desolate place to scrabble away on such a hopeless project?

The question asked was answered easily enough. Bitterly I recalled the vainglorious dreams that had induced me, together with my wife and youngest daughter, to come to this place Norwegians call their South Coast, a barren clump of rocks flung into the northernmost edge of the inhospitable waters of the North Sea.

1

I picked up a piece of paper at random. Taking a pencil, I placed it just to the right of the last written word and pushed it slowly across the page, inscribing as I went a string of symmetrical loops that, if not exactly dynamic prose, were at least a passable representation of Palmer Method Lesson 27 on the cursive *e*. Upon reaching the bottom of the page, I put down the pencil and stared intently at the scribbles.

The effort failing to produce anything useful, I closed my eyes and covered my face with my hands. In this position I remained for some time until the sound of my head striking the table interrupted my train of thought. I picked up another sheet of paper and began reading.

The first wave spun the kayak around like a top. Around and around it went, once, twice, three times. Face the waves! One strong paddle stroke.

The paddle! He looked across the water. There it was, bobbing six feet astern. It might as well have been in Greenland.

Wham! A collision. The boat shuddered convulsively and then was still. He peered into the fog. It was impenetrable. He tried to rock the kayak free. It would not budge. He scrunched down in the kayak. There was nothing to do but wait for the fog to lift. Two days later the paddle floated into the inlet at Hella. They never found the kayak.

Nadya tried to console her mother. "Mama?" she said softly, passing her arm around Trine's waist and drawing close.

"Yes, dear."

"You know how you and Dad are always talking about if it gets to where he doesn't know which side is up, and the only choice would be to put him in a nursing home? Only you don't know if you could do it? Well, now you don't have to worry. Or about the ashes either, whether to bury them at home under the maple, or scatter them in Wellfleet like Grandpa..."

"Stop!"

It was Trine. Absorbed in my reading, I had not heard her come downstairs. I looked at her sternly. Interruption of a reciting author was an indiscretion of the first order, and beloved though she was, a rebuke was in order. There being no immediate response from the better half, I considered the addition of a verbal reprimand, but demurred. Perhaps I was being a little harsh. After all, her interruption could just as easily have been the result of an uncontrollable urge to express pleasure at what she had just heard.

"The best is yet to come, my dear," I said proceeding on this assumption. "Shall I continue?"

"I've heard quite enough, thank you," she snapped. The urge, however great it may have been, was well controlled.

"Pretty snappy, huh?" I ventured hopefully.

"It's awful," she said, adding for emphasis. "I hate it."

"Then I presume, *my dear*, you don't want to hear the rest."

"You presume correctly."

"Missing then, the submarine?"

"Missing the submarine."

"As well as my daring escape?"

"That also."

"And the plane explosion, and the conspiracy, and the eggs?"

"Eggs?"

Had a tiny interest bud sprouted? Perhaps. Thus encouraged, I plunged forward with the plot.

"The president comes from Dumster. I am his doctor. A secret Nazi organization kidnaps me and replaces me with an imposter. The imposter tells the president that he has an enlarged prostate and that the only way to prevent cancer is to eat fifteen eggs every day. When the president's cholesterol goes way up, the imposter puts him on medicine to lower it. The medicine slows down his heart rate. The doctor inserts a pacemaker into the president. But the pacemaker is actually a defibrillator, which can stop the heart upon a remote signal. The secret Nazi organization demands five billion dollars to keep from activating the defibrillator. The president—"

"Stop!"

"But I haven't developed the whole idea. You see—"

"I've got a better idea."

"What is it?" I asked cautiously. I was not wholly persuaded by this sudden show of enthusiasm.

"Forget it."

"Forget the president? But he's crucial to what happens next."

"Forget the whole thing."

"I know it sounds a little rough, but I'm just getting started. This creative stuff takes time, you know."

"You're creative enough already. Let's go home."

Chapter 2

Greener Pastures

I came to Dumster ten years ago, emigrating from Berkeley, California, in search of the quiet life of a country doctor. It was quite a change for me, and my first year of practice was a difficult one. I kept a diary of that year, which some years later was published as a book. It was not a substantial work, but it did enjoy modest success in Vermont.

I am a sensitive person, and, as is common among people of sensitivity, a little bit of praise can go a long way. The effect of seeing my name in print was considerable. I took to wondering whether I should give up doctoring and become a serious writer. It was an agonizingly difficult question. On one side was the fame attendant upon being a renowned author. On the other was my devoted band of patients, who showered me with gratitude for even the slightest triumph. In short, the praise situation boiled down to this: writer—high quantity; doctor—high quality.

I often brooded about this question, sometimes leaning toward the thrill of a new career, sometimes favoring the security of the old. But I never did much more than think about it, and very likely never would have, except that one day the scales were tipped by a chance remark from one of my patients.

"Doc," he said. "I just read that book of yours. You know what I think?"

Thinking was not an activity I generally encouraged in my patients, but under the circumstances, I thought it reasonable to make an exception.

"No Fusswood," I replied. "What do you think?"

"I think you missed your calling."

To describe the effect of this remark as shocking would not be quite on the mark. Nor would it be strictly accurate to call it stupendous. There is only one word that really fits the bill. Cataclysmic.

4

This reaction to a remark by an ordinary patient may seem, even for a sensitive person, a bit excessive. But this was no ordinary patient. This was William Fusswood.

William Fusswood is a patient upon whom I have performed every conceivable test, for whom I have made every possible diagnosis, to whom I have administered every known remedy, and from whom I have extracted every drop of blood, sweat, and cash that was doctorly possible. William Fusswood is, in short, my best patient. And now he was saying, as casually as if he were commenting on the weather, that I am in the wrong line of work.

It was a pretty stiff broadside to the old applecart, and I spent the rest of the day wandering about in a dazed funk. When one of my patients confessed to taking vitamin E for his heart trouble, they say my only reply was "How nice." And I am alleged to have told some poor chap with lumbago he might be better off at the chiropractor's. I can't deny it. This page of my memory book remains a total blank.

Fortunately, when I turned down a second helping of strawberry shortcake at supper that night, Trine recognized that something was seriously amiss. She asked me what was the matter.

"You dummy," she said after I told her, explaining what to a less sensitive person would have been obvious—namely that Fusswood was not criticizing my doctoring, he was praising my writing.

This cast the matter in a whole new light. My equanimity restored, I asked myself the natural question. Was he right? Was there, lying dormant under the surface of Doctor Conger, a Dickens, a Tolstoy, an Arthur Conan Doyle? And remote as the possibility might be, was it fair to take the chance and deny the world what I had to offer for a mere handful of saved lives? No! Thundered self in reply. It was not!

Because writers, like doctors, are sensitive people, they need to have a responsible person who can watch over them. This is a person who is always supportive of their slightest accomplishments and who can ensure that they won't be hurt by behavior on the part of others that they might interpret as being critical. For the doctor, this role is fulfilled by a nurse. For the writer, it is his agent. Having made my decision, I immediately called my agent to tell her I was going to be writing another book. Of course, she was very excited at the news. She sounded a little unsure when I told her it was going to involve serious writing, but she encouraged me to keep at it anyway and said we could work out the details later on.

So it was that I found myself, after twenty-five years of sailing the lee, hauling in the mainsail, coming about, and setting off into the wind.

A new course taken is, well—a new course, and prudence demanded that I undertake it with care. Had I still been in California, it would have simply been a matter of going to the Tassajara Hot Springs for a Writers Total Immersion Retreat. But as Vermont offered no such opportunities, I had to take a more circuitous route.

First I went to the Dumster public library and took out a bunch of books about famous writers. I studied them carefully in search of the kind of important details someone planning to become a serious writer would need to know, such as where he did his best writing, and what kind of clothes inspired his prose. Then I set out to get some first hand observations of my own. I was fortunate in this respect, for right in my own neighborhood, there lived two actual famous authors, J. D. Salinger and Alexander Solzhenitsyn. Since the former had hidden himself deep in the woods, and the latter had surrounded his house with a big fence, I didn't actually talk with them, but by hanging out a lot at the Plainfield Country Store and the Cavendish Market, I did get to see each of them once.

This is what I learned.

Writing must be done in a place that no person in his right mind would voluntarily go. The less habitable the place, the better it is for writing.

The best time to write is during those hours when normal people are asleep. It should, under no circumstances, be done between the hours of nine and five. This is when creative powers are at a minimum.

A serious writer never uses a computer. The ideal writing device is an old typewriter with a few keys missing.

Serious writers wear bulky sweaters.

I bought a couple of sweaters, and I picked a stuffy corner up in our attic for my desk. While clearing it out, I made a great find. It was my father's old Smith Corona.

My father was an editor for the *New York Herald Tribune*. The Trib wasn't just a job for dad. The Trib was where he lived. And the Trib was where, on April 24, 1966, he died. Now if you looked at my father's death certificate, you would find listed under date, February 15, 1968, and under place, Pleasantville, New York. What the death certificate was referring to was that time when my father's body and soul formally separated, the former going down in the elevator at the *Reader's Digest* at a time when the latter chose to ascend. For all practical purposes, however, the two had been totally estranged ever since that fatal day in April. You see, soul never forgave body for quitting the Trib. It considered the matter a clear case of abandoning the post and was furious beyond words. Body, however, had no choice in the matter. For that was the date the paper shut down its presses for the last time. Unfortunately, when the paper closed, body became so utterly depressed that it couldn't even talk about it. Thus, body never bothered to explain the situation to soul. Hence the rupture.

I grew up in the town of Pleasantville, New York. Pleasantville was just the kind of town you would expect it to be. It was a quiet unassuming town, not given to great excesses or flights of imagination. It was a town where boys wanted to be just like other boys, and we all wanted to be just like our fathers, for whose every act we had an unquestioning reverence.

The time of my upbringing was the fifties. It was a time of traditional values, a time when in the morning the men went off to work, and the women stayed home. And a time when in the evening, the men went off to the bar, and the women brought them back home.

Accordingly, to a young boy, his intoxicated father represented the pinnacle of male manhood. After baseball and kick the can, bragging about our fathers' exploits under the influence was our most popular pastime. Tony Cannizzaro's father, for example, inspired by a pair of six-packs, once drove his fifty-two Ford into Opperman's Pond to see if it would really stay afloat with the windows rolled up. And Benny Johnson's dad, upon leaving Foley's Bar and Grill one night, stopped to relieve himself on a nearby telephone pole, which pole turned out to be the left leg of Police Chief Martin. These dads were real men.

When my dad got drunk, he fell asleep.

I would have had a childhood of immeasurable suffering were it not for my father's old typewriter. That Smith-Corona saved me from the inevitable ridicule and ultimate rejection attendant upon a kid whose dad was deemed a dud.

On the cover of the typewriter was a small dent. This, my father had told me, resulted from a stray bullet that had given him a close call when he was in Paris covering the German invasion. I took this raw material and refined it over the years, until by the time I was fourteen my father had saved an entire squadron with

7

his typewriter, holding it up to deflect a hand grenade tossed into his foxhole, grabbing the grenade, and then tossing it back into the enemy bunker just before it exploded. It was a great story, and even though it was committed under the influence of sobriety, it was my ticket to peer approval.After my father died, my mother told me that the famous dent was actually so ordinary, that neither she or my father had any notion whatsoever of its origin.

This was a pretty startling revelation. I had always trusted my dad to be on the level about such things. Not that he always told the truth. Like all parents, my father lied to me on a regular basis. But these were useful lies, to protect me from things I shouldn't know, like how much longer it was going to be until we got to Uncle Kyril's or that we were in a situation where the truth might give me the impression that he didn't know what he was doing. But my father never lied for pleasure. He was an editor.

Which is why this typewriter, symbolizing the one act of whimsy in a life dedicated to the minding of p's and q's, seemed the perfect vehicle for drawing out my creative fancy. So I went up into the attic early in the morning and again late at night, and for hours on end I rested my hands on the keys awaiting the emancipation of my imagination. Twice I felt something tingling in my fingertips, and I pounded away furiously. But all that came out was an order for Milk of Magnesia and a prescription for Valium.

I consulted Trine. She said I needed to get away from the influence of Doctor Conger. She suggested her parent's cottage at Bjorøya. As Bjorøya was, to anyone but a Norwegian, better suited for a penal colony than a vacation spot, it seemed the perfect site. At its mere mention, I could feel prose bubble up in my brain like lava from a volcano.

But for one matter, I was ready to be on the way. It was the matter of my practice.

Chapter 3
Setting Sail

Coming into Dumster from the north, the first business one encounters is Bascomb Sunoco, Chet's—as both it and its proprietor, Chester Arthur Bascomb, are more generally known. If you buy gas at Chet's you pay a little more than at the Jiffy Mart, and if you get your car repaired, it costs a lot less than up in Lebanon.

It is fashionable, in today's business world, to structure one's organization along the lines of the most complex of geometrical shapes, such as the pentangle, the tetrahedron, or the double ellipse. It is considered a sign of sophistication. As Bascomb Sunoco is not much in the sophistication department, it has adopted instead for its role model, a more simple form. The flagpole.

At the base is Willy Hunter, the most contemporary in a long line of dispensers of gasoline. Willy is a good lad, and he is usually equal to the task at hand, excepting only the dispensing of directions to those out-of-towners who, depending upon such notions as so many miles, or such-and-such sign, are unable to recognize the navigational landmarks upon which Willy relies. Such as Lyman's field, which, as it now sports the Grand Union, has lost much of its agricultural character. Or Shute Road, Shute being the dominant lineage of the populace residing along a thoroughfare upon whose sign post are written the arcane letters, TOWN HWY 24.

Above Willy is Armand Leblanc, a cantankerous old French Canadian who has been Chet's mechanic since its inception. Armand's love for the company of engines is matched only by his disdain for the species that created them. To watch Armand at work cooing softly to an aged Olds or exulting in the roar of a nicely tuned Corvette is enough to give one serious pause before he again applies to any member of the internal combustion family, the sobriquet inanimate.

Above Armand is Chet. Although Chet is the titular head of the business, the pole does not end with him. There is one more Bascomb Sunocian. Known generally as Boss, she is perched securely at the top and looks down upon all her charges with maternal devotion. She is Chet's wife Rachel. Rachel keeps the books, and Rachel is the only person who has the faintest idea if Bascomb Sunoco is making good money, barely breaking even, or about to go under, all of which options it has exercised regularly since 1946, when Chet opened the station after returning from the war.

In the twenty years that Emmeline Talbot Memorial Hospital has been open, the chair's seat on the Board of Trustees has been occupied by a single body—Chet's. By day up to his armpits in grime and clatter, Chet is fascinated by the genteel world of directorship. Chet loves nothing better than to sit back of an evening, a heavily tomed annual report before him, and wax eloquent about reserved balances, capital emoluments, and accounts inscrutable. Equally content is he to listen for hours on end as architects and advisors and attorneys prattle on about their favored scheme for the welfare of Emmeline Talbot Memorial, schemes that, should any one of them walk into Chet's and offer them up for his consideration, Chet would him declare nutty as a jaybird and throw him out on his ear.

Chet is a good chair. He runs his meetings fairly, and he has an uncanny sense of when it is time to move the question. Unencumbered by any interest in the substance, Chet rules by tone. A tendency to drone, a shifting of the chairs, a hint of acrimony, and the subject is closed up tight as a drum. "She's all tuned up and ready to go" is the standard pronouncement with which he signifies that the deliberations have reached their apex, and it is time to move on.

This is not to say Chet looks unfavorably upon debate. On the contrary, he loves a good verbal hullabaloo, and the more trivial the issue, the better. He once kept going for three board meetings a discussion on the question regarding next to which of her favorite haunts the tree donated by Elmer Knox in memory of his beloved wife Harriet should be planted. One side had advocated the emergency room, which she had regularly frequented. The other said it should be outside Room 102, where she died.

Chet has abundant good sense, and he has, as well, an excellent sense of nonsense. Thus it was with some apprehension that I anticipated his response, when I met with the trustees to inform them that their beloved Doctor Conger would be taking an indefinite leave to pursue literary aspirations.

In making my case, I touched eloquently upon the point I considered crucial to its comprehension—the point of one's need to find oneself. As this was a concept with which Dumster was not much familiar, I illuminated it with a homily about how a doctor was like a good plow horse, you got more mileage out of him if you let him out to graze now and then than if you worked him to death.

Following my presentation there was an awkward silence, which Chet terminated with the following words.

"Pretty dumb idea."

If Chet were to have amplified this statement—which he didn't—it might have gone something like this.

You've already got a job.

Which, I must concede is a good point. But there comes a time in some people's lives when, as they are pressing their noses ever tightly to the grindstone, they hear, through the din and the clatter, a call. It is a clarion call. And a clarion call is one that will not be denied. It is a call that must be answered. Chet's ears, tuned to a different frequency than mine, did not often receive such calls, so I could understand his disapprobation at the time. I had no doubt, however, that on that future day when, my literary fame firmly established, I returned in glory, the notes would ring in his ears with a resounding clarity, and his view of the matter would be altered. As to the question of exactly when that day would be—a question he seemed unduly eager to pursue—I could not exactly say. In the meantime, there was, as he noted, the point of my patients.

Sensitive as I was to my own needs, I was not indifferent to those of my patients. I knew how difficult it would be for them to wake up each morning knowing that, should a touch of indigestion lay claim to being a heart attack, or an ache behind the ear develop tendencies toward cancer, they would not have their trusted Doc to see them through. They would need some other port, inferior as it might be, in which they could weather the coming storms.

Excepting the surgeons, who flitted like migratory birds among Emmeline Talbot and two other hospitals, the only other doctor in Dumster was Dale Hurbalife.

In his prime, Hurbalife was a brilliant neurologist who had won acclaim for his research on the inhabitants of a remote South Pacific island where everyone was lefthanded. Charles Darwin, who had first described this phenomenon in *The Voyage of the Beagle,* ascribed it to inbreeding; but Doctor Hurbalife, while there on vacation, discovered that a small band of emigrants from a neighboring island, after living there for many years, had converted from their former righthanded state to southpaw. Further, he found that a local species of ant, which the natives consumed in great quantities as a delicacy, had the habit, when returning home at the end of a day's forage, of straying off its path—and always to the left.

Doctor Hurbalife's observations generated intense interest at the Pentagon, which generously funded his research on the island for many years. Before his work could reach fruition, however, the local sultan was overthrown by Marxist revolutionaries, and the contract was canceled.

Nonetheless, Hurbalife's efforts did not go unrewarded. In 1974 he was named Dean of the Johns Hopkins School of Public Health and moved to Baltimore, where he spent several productive years studying the mating habits of the monarch butterfly.

Like many gazing from the summit over the valley of medicine, Doctor Hurbalife often pined for the halcyon fields below. Truth be known, Hurbalife had never done any actual tilling of the fields himself. He had traveled straight from his training to the National Institutes of Health, where he resided until his sojourn in the South Pacific, and this fact may have added substantially to the appeal of such a life. Be that as it may, it was not long after I came to Dumster that Doctor Hurbalife, by then in his early seventies and intent upon living out the remainder of his days in country quietude, arrived in town to set up shop.

It may have been a case of too many years of the rarified air of academe or perhaps too many ant casseroles. Whatever the cause, there could be no doubt that by the time he made the trip from Baltimore to Dumster, the screws that held Doctor Hurbalife's engine in place had loosened a few turns. Raised on the rules of modern medicine, Hurbalife had become a devotee of the archaic. Homeopathy was his guiding light, and herbs his therapeutic staple. Thus did a man who had sworn by the law of the randomized double blind plunge into the blind domain of the random. Doctor Hurbalife was a quack.

The line that separates a physician who practices medicine to its ultimate from one who debases it by quackery is a fine one. So fine, in fact, that it can easily be crossed on a regular basis, and would be were it not for our strict adherence to a vital tenet that separate the hocus from the pocus and keeps the witch out of the doctor.

A doctor never recommends anything that can be taken without a prescription.

Unwilling to let Doctor Hurbalife loose on the crop I had so carefully cultivated, and reluctant to take a chance with a mail-order doctor, I was at a loss for what to do until Trine had said, "What about Sandra Smart?"

Sandra Smart had gone to medical school at Dartmouth. She had been assigned to my office as part of her community medical experience, a program that gives the next generation a chance to see the old natives in their natural habitat. Although it is intended primarily as comic relief from the drudgery of modern medicine, Sandra had taken a great interest in my practice. She was a lively, friendly soul, and I had enjoyed having her with me. Even after she went off to Maine for her residency, we kept in touch. I wrote to her to see if she might want to kick off her career in Dumster. She said yes.

I figured it would be a difficult job to sell the trustees on the idea of bringing in some whippersnapper fresh off the vine, so I pushed my points pretty hard. I laid it on thick about the value of a fresh perspective and someone who was up to snuff on all the most recent advances in medicine. I was quite persuasive. Still, there were plenty of furrowed brows until I mentioned Doctor Smart. I emphasized that, as she had been personally trained by me, they would be getting the closest thing to Doc Conger without having his actual flesh and blood. Upon this final argument, even Chet Bascomb was forced to concede.

"Smart?" he said. "Hmmm. I remember her. You do what you got to, Doc. We'll manage."

Thus reassured, I embarked upon my journey, promising to all that my absence would not be for long. Six months, a year—maybe two. Whatever it took.

It took three weeks.

This placed me in something of a dilemma. To return so soon would be unfair to Doctor Smart, who had barely had time to get her bags unpacked. One the other hand, I was in no mood to twiddle my thumbs on a pile of Norwegian rocks. Flubbing the chance at flowing prose, I was itching to prove my creative worth by once again applying pen to the paper of my former favored medium. The pad. I stewed over the predicament at great length but could see no solution. As usual, Trine came to my rescue.

"Why not take Sandra on as a partner?" she suggested.

It was the perfect solution. My practice, if not busy enough for two, could certainly suffice for one and a half. And with the spare time, I could pursue my literary inclinations albeit at a more modest pace.

I wrote to Sandra outlining my proposal. She readily assented, and without further ado, we packed our bags and headed for home.

Chapter 4

Reunion

It was a Sunday afternoon in late September. I sat in my living room looking out the window at the setting rays of summer. It was a peaceful time. It was a time for quiet reflection, as I tallied up my blessings at the end of one week and gathered strength for the beginning of another.

The stately maple that graced our front yard was directly in my line of vision. Its fireball fall hairdo, which outshone even the sun at this time of year, forced it into my attention and lent to my meditation an arboreal tone.

How pleasant are trees, I thought. Quiet and unassuming, humble to a fault, trees really are quite nice to have around. They give us, freely and without reserve, oxygen, shelter, heat, and a place to hang the swing. Generous to a fault, they could, were they not so modest, lay a pretty good claim to the title of man's best friend.

Admittedly, trees do have an unsettling tendency to stake a claim anywhere they see fit, without the slightest regard for the possibility that it might be just the place for a shopping mall, or, if they had set up camp just a little to the right, they would not have spoiled the view. But other than these minor indiscretions, trees are a very accommodating lot. One could hardly ask for a better neighbor.

If you live in the city, where trees are usually cast with the homeless, you probably don't think too much about trees. Around Dumster, however, they can't be avoided. The poor things are all over the place, looking wistfully at you when you read the morning paper, or making as if they wanted to make a break for the next planet every time you fire up your wood stove. It's enough to put a sensitive person quite off his feed.

Rubbish, you say? Trees don't have feelings. Let me tell you about our maple. It is a robust middle-aged specimen that has lived on our street for upwards of one hundred years, a distinction in recognition of which, the street is named. The previous owner of our house had let it pretty much have the run of the place, and when we moved in, we found it to be a most obstreperous creature. In the fall it would drop leaves willy-nilly in the gutter. In the summer it would drape its branches all over the tomatoes. And in winter it was forever dumping snow on our heads when we exited the front door. It was a tree in need of discipline.

First I cut off the top to check its unbridled growth. Then I trimmed its errant extremities. Finally I drove a hook into the trunk to hold one end of a hammock. I attached the other end to the house. It was there, in place of the living room chair, that I took my warm weather repose.

In the fall I would remove the hammock for winter storage, and in the spring I would bring it back out again. About the third summer, I noticed that the hammock was taut when I strung it up. The next year I couldn't attach it at all. I figured the hammock had shrunk and bought a replacement exactly like the old one. But the new one didn't fit either. I puzzled over this a bit, but soon forgot the matter.

Forgot it, that is, until five years ago, when, while mowing the lawn I discovered that I could no longer fit the mower in the space between the tree and the fence that marked our boundary with the adjacent churchyard. Next year the space was even narrower. By then it was obvious. Our maple was trying to escape. It was fleeing our yard for the sanctity of the North Church Cemetery.

Such behavior by trees is not at all unusual. Ask any farmer. He will tell you that, even on a windless day, when he hits the first blow to drive a tap into a sugar maple, or his chainsaw takes the first bite out of a firewood destined ash, he will often feel a slight tremor from the trunk and hear a rustling in the leaves. The tree is shuddering.

To alienate oneself from his resident arboreal is not good policy. In our neck of the woods, it is one of those things that simply is not done. So I have patched things up with our maple. The hook is out, the pruning shears are gone, and the lowest limb now sports a bird feeder. And I am pleased to report that the outward movement of our maple has stopped. Which is as it should be.

One can't help but benefit by living next to a tree. It is, I suspect, such cohabitation that gives to the people of Dumster an edge over those who must rely for moral guidance on the Sears Tower or the World Trade Center. Like the trees upon whom they lean, the people of Dumster are modest in their demands and grateful for that which they have rather than envious of that which they do not. Similarly in emulation of their sylvan mentors, Dumsterians are restrained in their expression of feelings.

Thus, I did not expect an ostentatious welcome upon my return home. There would be no banners on Main Street. No red carpet at the hospital entrance. A warm smile, a hearty handshake, perhaps a few flowers on my desk from someone whose exaltation could not be contained. I expected nothing more.

I was not disappointed. Margaret Stone, the person who, for the past ten years had been in charge of holding my toes to the line, and, when despite her efforts they wandered off to the side, kept the wolves at bay, met me as I entered the office in a manner that would have done honor to even the most proper of the Main Street oaks.

"Maggie," I said commencing the address I had prepared for the occasion. "It's good to be back. This is the place I belong. These are the people I should be with. This is what I should be doing."

It was a good speech, short and to the point, but with a just enough of the philosophical to give it some punch.

"Mr. Fusswood is your first patient," replied Maggie.

"Maggie," I said. "That's what I love about you. That's what I love about Dumster. No nonsense. No hoopla. Eloquence in understatement."

"He will be in at nine-thirty."

The words were few, but they were more than enough to show she cared and was glad to have me back. One among them would have sufficed.

Fusswood.

Fusswood. It is a name tied with mine in a bond so strong that no earthly force could rend it asunder. *Fusswood and Doc,* a pair indelibly scribed in the annals of doctor-patient relationships. *Fusswood and Doc,* forever together. *Fusswood and Doc,* two as one.

We all start out on the road of life with the expectation that, should we play our cards right, not wander too far from the highway, and receive at least a fair share of the luck, our tenure on the coil should be a long and a healthy one. This philosophy, desirable as it may appear at the outset, has one major drawback that renders it totally unsuitable for the journey. It ill equips us for dealing with the slings and arrows that inevitably assault us as we progress further down the way.

Setbacks are an essential part of the human experience. And a life well lived is a life in which those setbacks can be incorporated with as much—and I use the word not in its literal, but in its contrasting sense—*pleasure* as can be extracted from it. A life must be able to suffer as well in sickness as it is to prosper in health.

Among the many satisfactions derived from the practice of medicine, easily the most rewarding is helping people to cope with this predicament, teaching them that to avoid the ruts is not only futile, but misses the whole point of the trip, which is not—as some would think—to sit idly back and enjoy the scenery. It is to grab a firm hold on the wheel, to plow relentlessly ahead, and to take the worst it has to offer without complaint.

The means by which a person inexperienced in the matter of suffering gains the necessary skill is to become a patient. And although people are born, patients are made, and nowhere is the skill of a doctor more in evidence than in how she creates the latter from the former. Fusswood, before he met me, had no more idea of how to be a patient than of how to concoct the elixir of eternal youth, but through a series of circumstances that, as I have related them before, I will not repeat here, I relieved him of that heavy cloak of invincibility with which he had borne himself through life up to that point and clothed him in a garment more suitable for the remainder of his journey.

It being only nine o'clock, I had about an hour and a half to kill, so I wandered out to the cafeteria for tea. When I came back, Fusswood was waiting. Considering the occasion, he looked remarkably calm.

"Fusswood, my boy," I said shaking his hand. "It's good to be back. This is the place I belong. These are the people I should be with. This is what I should be doing."

"You're late," said Fusswood.

Whether my mouth actually dropped completely open at this point, I cannot say for sure, but of this I have no doubt—there was a sudden descent of my lower mandible. And it was more than a few notches. For I was shocked. This was hardly the response I expected to hear from my most loyal and trusted upon reuniting with his favorite healer.

"Fusswood," I said, "I'm shocked."

"One hour to be precise," he replied coolly. "I presume you have an explanation."

This was incredible! Insolence beyond the pale. "An explanation?" I sputtered. "You *presume?* What on earth—"

"Doc," he said, flushing hotly, "I can't afford to wait around like this. My time is valuable." He stopped to collect himself. "At least to me it is." Although he was now more conciliatory, it was too late to close what was becoming a breach of Red Sea proportions.

There are many things that we do for our patients for which we never expect to get credit, but which we do because we are the kind of people we are. Like interrupting our practice to pack off to some remote tropical island, just so we can learn more about the latest in medical advances. Or dropping everything to run down to Washington to ensure that congress will guarantee every American the right to see his doctor without worrying about the doctor getting paid.

There is one, however, among these sacrificial acts before which all others pale. One which, if one wanted to pick that which symbolizes what makes a doctor tick, it would take first prize, hands down and no doubt about it.

Some—the whiners mostly—have claimed that when some poor patient has been trying for months to see me about a terrible affliction, and then he finds himself cooling his heels for hours on end while I am in the cafeteria having tea, that I am callously indifferent to his plight. Nothing could be further from the truth.

Few things cause me greater distress than the knowledge that there are patients desperately awaiting my healing hand for whom I must yet stay that hand. But stay it I must. For there is an axiom that, if you gain nothing else from this work, you should at least take this one away with you. It is that important.

Waiting is fundamental to the therapeutic process.

Imagine this. One morning, while staying in a motel in a distant town, you awaken with a twitch in your side. You attempt to ignore it, but it persists. Within minutes it develops into terminal cancer. In terror, you flee to the nearest doctor's office. Bolting through the door, you are struck with a sense of foreboding. You can't quite put your finger on it, but something is not right. Before you can collect your thoughts, a nurse comes up to you and says, "The doctor will see you now." She hustles you off to a room. The doctor is there. You state your complaint. The doctor examines you. She declares you to be well.

At this juncture your only sensation should be one of immense relief. Nothing so perks up one's day as a narrow escape from death. And yet you remain vaguely discontented. You leave. On your way back to the motel it hits you. Something was wrong. *Very* wrong. What was it?

You review the events. You arrived. You were seen. You left. It was easy. That was it! It was *too* easy! Where were the hordes of devoted patients waiting with lunch pail and toothbrush to see their beloved healer? Somewhere else!

Or consider that special occasion you wish to celebrate with a night of dining out. Is it the closest fast food emporium that you choose for the honor? It is not. Rather, you head for your favorite romantic hideaway. You arrive. You take a seat. The waiter, aptly named, comes up. You wish to order? You do not. The waiter leaves. You gaze about. You exchange glances. You chat. The atmosphere develops. The waiter returns. Perhaps a drink? You consider. And so it goes. The pace—unhurried, each step—considered, every detail—savored.

Seeing a doctor is no different. Before you and she can dine at the table of your complaint, the mood must be right. When you come to the doctor, you may be happy or angry or bored or burdened with any one of a number of emotions not at all suitable for the occasion. Your doctor, knows this, and she makes every attempt to prepare you for what she has to offer. First she places you in the waiting room, where you share with the other supplicants your hopes and fears of that which lies ahead. This provides enlightenment. Then, when you finally enter the examination room, you don a paper sack, ridding yourself, thereby, of your worldly persona. Now you are purified. The last step completes the transformation. You are gradually cooled down until your body reaches a temperature suitable for hibernation. Like a good white wine, a patient is best served slightly chilled.

Thus readied, you should, by the time the doctor arrives, have achieved *état théraputique,* that blessed state wherein you are eager to take as your immediate and only hope whatever the doctor has to offer.

For those skeptics who might claim the need for further proof on this point, I ask consideration of the following incident, which, because of its import, I will relate in its entirety.

James Kneeland was, despite a touch of asthma, an obstreperous prostate, and a defective hip, a robust seventy-five-year-old. He had just returned from a trip to the Holy Land and was coming in for a checkup. His appointment being for ten, it was with no little surprise that I received Maggie when she came out to the cafeteria at quarter of eleven to tell me that he was ready to see me. I was about to let Maggie know that her intrusion was not quite *comme il faut,* but something in her look made me think better of it. Hurriedly finishing my tea, I accompanied her back to the office where I found Mister Kneeland to be in such a condition as to excuse Maggie's extraordinary behavior.

Reclined upon the waiting room floor, it was apparent that however he had been equipped at the onset of his visit, Mr. Kneeland was now utterly deficient in two of the accoutrements one ordinarily brings on an outing to the doctor—namely heartbeat and respiration.

After a flurry of activity that returned Mister Kneeland to a more acceptable state, he was bundled off to the intensive care unit, where he subsequently made an uneventful recovery from his heart attack.

What would have happened had I seen Mister Kneeland at the appointed time, congratulated him on his good health, and sent him promptly packing? Quarter to eleven would have found him well on his way, not home but to a rather more distant location, return from which would have been problematic indeed.

Something was obviously amiss with Fusswood. This was not the Fusswood who, at my slightest command, would leap unquestioning into the most treacherous of tests. This was not the Fusswood who, if proffered from my hand, would swallow without hesitation the most poisonous of potions. This was not the Fusswood who worshipped the very ground upon which I walked. This was not Fusswood!

Was it the untoward effect of some pill? The first sign of brain fever? Or was it rather an unconscious reaction to my prolonged absence? This seemed most likely. It would not have been unnatural that under such circumstances Fusswood might harbor feelings of rejection, feelings which could, if unchecked, develop into resentment. Fusswood was, after all, a patient and therefore not always in control of his emotions. I, his doctor, could understand this. It was a time, not for recriminations, but for healing.

"Fusswood," I said, "I understand. You are hurting. But I am back, and all will be well. Sit down and tell me your troubles. All of them."

Fusswood flushed. "Uh—I don't know—I mean—You see—" He stopped, overcome with emotion.

"I know it's difficult. I have been gone for so long, and there are so many things we need to discuss. Do not worry, Fusswood. My time is your time. Unburden yourself."

"It's not about me, Doc," he replied slowly. "It's about you."

I placed a comforting hand on his shoulder. "There, there, Fusswood. I understand. You are worried that in my absence, I might have lost interest in you. A natural feeling. Let me assure you. My attachment is unabated. I am still your Doc of old."

"That's just it, Doc. You see, while you were gone, I had to see Sandr—er, Doctor Smart, and she—" Fusswood hesitated. He appeared unsure how to proceed.

I tried to help him. "I know. She isn't like me. But she is a good doctor nonetheless, and I'm sure she did you no irreparable harm. Anyway, that's all water over the dam. I'm back, and I'm here for you, and that's all that matters."

"—is different, Doc. And she—" He flushed bright red and stopped, again too agitated to speak.

Why was Fusswood so flustered? Something was clearly causing him great distress. Could it be—impossible! Still, a human spirit in distress is susceptible, and the temptation—painful as it might be, I had to find out.

"Fusswood," I said quietly. "Did something happen between you and Doctor Smart while I was away. Did she perhaps—" The blood that had precipitously rushed to Fusswood's face at the mention of Doctor Smart, now just as suddenly departed. His lips quivered as he tried to speak, but no words came out. The ground upon which I was treading was obviously sensitive. I began again, this time on a less direct tack. "While I was gone, did you have an—uh—*experience* with Doctor Smart? Something difficult to talk about? Something—unpleasant? Tell me. Please. I assure you, if you can get it off your chest, you will feel much better."

It often happens that in the course of her activities, a doctor must inflict pain upon her patient. To the extent that it furthers the end of ultimate cure, it is a normal part of the doctor-patient relationship.

The possibility that a doctor could abuse this relationship seems at face value absurd, but, Truth be known, there are a few bad eggs even in the doctor basket, and a prudent patient should be on the alert in the event, however unlikely, that he might be in the hands of one.

The doctor who sticks a needle into a patient's body without subsequently either withdrawing something from or instilling something into it, is an example of one such type. (An exception is made for neurologists, who are in the habit of administering pinpricks to their patients on a regular basis. They are excused on the grounds that neurologists are a little peculiar.)

Another is the doctor who, in answer to repeated inquiries from her patient as to the nature of the affliction in question, responds, "It's nothing to worry about," thereby ensuring that said patient will immediately sink into utter despair over what he reasonably assumes to be a condition so horrible that the doctor cannot even speak its name.

Worst of all is the doctor who, on grounds that nothing can be found wrong, refuses to administer treatment, thus instilling in her patient feelings of shame and inadequacy and reducing substantially the probability that the patient will seek attention for any subsequent complaint.

"Oh no!" Fusswood exclaimed shaking his head vigorously. "That's not it, Doc. That's not it at all. "I like Doctor Smart. I like her a lot. I like her a *real* lot!"

Talk about barking up the wrong tree. I wasn't even in the right forest. But what could have been more natural? Thrown together as they were, a sense of abandonment on Fusswood's part, a strong desire for acceptance on Doctor Smart's. It was chemistry of a most combustible sort. Nonetheless, it was inexcusable- on both their parts.

I eyed Fusswood sternly. "Tell—me—what—happened!" I commanded.

Fusswood looked at me blankly.

"Your relationship with Doctor Smart. When you said that you liked her—"

Fusswood started. My drift appeared to have reached shore.

"Doc!" he protested. "Not that way. I like her as my *doctor.* That's all! Believe me."

Though distressed, he betrayed no sign of dissembling. His denial appeared to be genuine.

"Of course. As a doctor. And a fine doctor she is. A fine *young* doctor. Why with a little experience—"

"That's what I wanted to talk to you about, Doc. You see, I was wondering—"

"If I would consider keeping her on as an associate. An excellent suggestion. It is a point I myself have considered at some length. My practice has grown considerably in the past several years, thanks," I nodded in acknowledgment, "in no small part to the devoted attendance of patients like yourself. It is indeed time for me to take on an associate. You will be pleased to know that I have offered the position to Doctor Smart, and she has accepted. You can be comfortable, therefore, in the knowledge that if, for any reason, I am unavailable, you will have her to back me up- although I assure you," I added hastily, for he was again showing signs of disquiet, "that unless I am forced to be absent from Dumster, no complaint will be too trivial, no schedule too full, and no hour to importune when it comes to the needs of Fusswood."

Fusswood appeared strangely unmoved. "She already told me she was staying, Doc," he said. "So I was thinking—what with you just getting back, and being so busy and all, maybe it would be easier if I kept seeing her for now—unless, of course, there was a real emergency, and she wasn't around. Naturally I'd call you then."

Having blurted this last speech out as if ridding himself of some terrible burden, Fusswood looked at me expectantly.

It was a delicate situation. I paused to collect my thoughts before I spoke again. When I did, my words were carefully chosen.

"Thank you Fusswood," I began—graciously, but with enough hint of severity to indicate that I considered the suggestion uncalled for. "Your offer is quite considerate. But unnecessary, I assure you. *Entirely* unnecessary. I expect to be able to handle all your needs myself."

"Sure, Doc. But—you see—I've sort of gotten used to Doctor Smart."

"Of course you have. And we have already discussed that subject, I believe. I am sure, however, that after a few visits with me, you will forget all about her."

"That's just it," he said. "I don't know if I *want* to forget. What I mean is—" he paused and looked me full in the face. "I think I'll stick with her. Not that I don't like you, too. And if she isn't around you're my number one backup. Like you said, we go back a long way. Anyway. I just wanted to drop back to say hello. Didn't mean to take up so much time. Your schedule must be pretty busy these days, what with all your old patients trying to get in to see you. So—welcome back to Dumster, Doc."

And with that, he gave me a quick salute, got up from the chair, and left.

Chapter 5
A Fall

I had expected that the taking up again of the profession I had recently abdicated would not be without its complications. Nonetheless, I was confident that the love and attention from my devoted patients would keep my spirits sufficiently buoyed to allow me to weather the storm without difficulty.

The experience with Fusswood, however, disturbed my equanimity, and it occasioned a lively, and at times acrimonious, debate among my sensibilities. Not surprisingly, it was sensitivity who spoke first, stating that the incident was nothing short of outright rejection, and responsibility for the fiasco lay squarely at the feet of judgment, who had carelessly led them all astray. To this proposition readily assented both a resentful ambition and an outraged conscience, the former mostly pouting and the latter muttering about how no one ever listened to her, and if only she had been consulted in the first place, this whole thing would never have happened. Then they all chimed in—guilt, anger, even pride, who gave an impassioned speech in which he declared that the situation was a clear case of while the cat was away, the mice had been dancing on the table, and the cat now being back, should put an end to the monkey business forthwith. Fortunately it was reason who prevailed in the end, pointing out that Fusswood could hardly have been any less unsettled than I at this turn of events, and as such could not be held responsible for his actions. Time, it assured, would certainly heal the breach.

The ensuing days, however, gave indication that this universal balm might be slow to work its effect. My office was not filled with hordes of patients eager to place themselves once again at my disposal, and my days were occupied by much resorting of files, numerous cups of teas, and extended reviews of the medical literature. On one particularly languid day, during which my sole activities consisted of morning break, lunch, and afternoon tea, I broached the subject with Maggie, wondering if, unlikely as it seemed, word of my return had not been sufficiently spread.

Maggie, in most apologetic tones, replied that the situation was entirely her fault. She had thought it best not to wear me out before I had my feet under me again and had intentionally kept my schedule light. In due time, she assured me, she would loose the floodgates. Until then I should relax in preparation for the grueling days that were sure to come.

Her speech was reassuring, but by the third week, after I had given repeated hints as to my readiness again to do battle, without any apparent effect, I became suspicious. And then an event happened, so conclusive as to remove any doubt about the state in which my practice lay.

"Mister Sotwell called this morning," were Maggie's exact words that fateful morning. "He says he must see you. I put him in at nine-thirty."

I gaped at Maggie in horror. Her words had hit me like a thunderbolt. I knew now what earlier I had only suspected. My practice, the carefully crafted creation of a decade's work, was destroyed. My career in Dumster was over. I was done for. Finished. Kaput.

How is it, you may ask, dear reader, that the announcement I am about to see a patient desperately seeking my care, would throw me into such a state of consternation? Am I perhaps being a little *too* sensitive? Well let me just say this, and then I will present the case and let you be the judge, confident that having heard the particulars, you will render a verdict in my favor. Had Archibald Peabody Sotwell been the last patient on the face of the earth, and I the last doctor, and he at my door dying, and me with the cure, I could, in clear conscience, shut the door in his face.

There is a principle, axiomatic to the profession, but not generally shared with the public, that pursuant to my pledge, I must now break ranks to divulge.

The success of a doctor's practice has less to do with the quality of the doctor than it does with the quality of those upon whom she practices.

Like the teacher who can do little with the ignorant student, or the preacher who wastes his words on the heathen, a doctor's greatest healing powers will come but to naught in the hands of an unresponsive patient.

It follows therefore, that the single best measure of a physician's practice is her ability to maintain a vigorous crop of patients, a never-ending task that requires not only the nurturing of the good, but also the weeding out of the bad—lest they contaminate the rest of the lot.

The reader might reasonably suppose from the above that this Mister Sotwell chap was some hopeless reprobate. Such, however, was not the case. As a person, Archibald Peabody Sotwell was not disagreeable. He paid his bills promptly, and his demeanor was both cheerful and friendly. As a patient, however, Sotwell was a horse of quite another color.

On the principle that it is best to begin at the beginning, I will commence with our first encounter. It was during my second week in Dumster. I was in the emergency room when Archibald Peabody arrived via ambulance. The proximate cause of our introduction was the patient's rapid descent from a height of considerable magnitude, and he was preceded by a large entourage in such a state of consternation that I was convinced it would be a case for all the king's horses and all the king's men.

Early in the course of my examination, it became apparent that his was a most striking case. In the first place, despite the violence of his fall, Archibald Peabody was, save for a slight cut over his left eye and a small bump below his right knee, virtually unhurt. In the second, it turned out that he was engaged, at the time of this fall, in the act of riding a horse. That someone living in the country should incur injury during this activity might not seem of much note, and ordinarily it would not have been, save for the additional fact that the particular location in which the fall occurred was that stretch of land between Archibald Peabody's upstairs bedroom and his front door.

The circumstances that lead to a grown man falling down a flight of stairs while mounted on his horse—who, I might add, did not fare nearly so well as his rider and had to be summarily dis-patched—can be easily explained by one other observation that no one considered singular at all, since it had been, for the past seventy years, synonymous with the name of Archibald Peabody Sotwell. Archibald Peabody was drunk.

Before proceeding further, I should explain that at the time of my arrival in Dumster, I was freshly sprung from the last in a succession of those formidable castles of healing that go by the name of medical centers, a deceptively innocuous title that conceals their real function within the profession—that being to provide refuge for the most secretive, and therefore most powerful, of the members of the species medico sapiens. The pajama doctors.

Although the reader may not know them by this name, he has, if he has ever spent any time within the walls of which I speak, seen them, for there they are everywhere. Clad in their telltale garb, they gather in small groups—in corridors, at nursing stations, and over the beds of patients. They speak in low tones and have serious looks on their faces. Should he chance to overhear their conversations, he would not understand them, for they speak in tongues incomprehensible to—and unintended for—the human ear. Their correspondence is with the mysterious machines that hum and flash and beep over the bodies of the creatures who lie beneath them, in concert with which they can one minute work great miracles and the next wreak horrible havoc.

After one has been a pajama doctor one has, upon emerging in the outside world, rather definite opinions about his ability to alter the lives of those entrusted to his care, with a special definiteness that by so doing, his alterations will be for the better.

My inspection complete, I tended to Archibald Peabody's wounds. Then I pointed out to him that his neck having managed to stay unbroken through this episode was no fault of his, and that in my opinion, his problems could be traced to an excessive fondness for intoxicating beverages, of which problem I would, should he consent, be most glad to rid him.

Archibald Peabody agreed with me wholeheartedly. Declaring loudly I was the best thing that had ever happened to him, he promised to place himself entirely in my hands, and swore on the spot, abstinence henceforth.

It is painful, even today, to recount the details of our subsequent relationship. No stone did I leave unturned in my attempts to set for Archibald Peabody a path sufficiently straight and a way appropriately narrow as to keep him on the wagon. Each time, my hold tight on the reins, our course would start out true, but invariably, soon after embarking upon our journey, Archibald Peabody would make a lurch to the side and, breaking his traces, fall head over teakettle back into the soup. Some period of wandering in the wilderness would then ensue, but eventually he would make his way to that place which is to the Dumster inebriate what Rome was to Caesar, Gola's Bar and Grill. There, after refreshing himself at length, he would regale his fellow travelers with an eloquent dissertation on the wonders of Doctor Conger, who, having saved his life more times than he could count, he swore to be the greatest doctor in the entire world. Following this encomium, he would announce that if anyone present wished to take issue with him, he would be most pleased to meet with him and the second of his choosing at a time and place of mutual convenience.

This method of upholding our mutual honors, archaic as it may seem, was no idle threat, for among his possessions, Archibald Peabody counted a handsome set of his great grandfather's German dueling swords, one of which, he regularly let known, had been in the grasp of said ancestor when he took his final breath.

None ever taking up the challenge, Archibald Peabody would down several more of his "usuals," whereupon, now fully fortified, he would march off to my office and declare that he was once again ready to place himself completely at my disposal.

This scene, repeated more often than I care to recall, became to the people of Dumster, a source of considerable entertainment. This was not so much owing to any malice on their part—in this the good townspeople are wholly lacking—as it was to their not being greatly blessed in the matter of diversions. Salutary as these pilgrimages may have been to the spirits of the Dumsterians, however, it was difficult for me to appreciate the gain, derived as it was primarily from stores in the warehouse of the dignity of Doctor Conger.

The final straw came about six months after his fall. Archibald Peabody had been in the throes of a particularly boisterous drunk when, staggering out of Gola's, he ran over Mildred Contremond, who was emerging from her son's general store with an armful of groceries. Mildred, by nature a quiet woman, was not much given to public speaking. Upon arising from the pavement, however, she turned upon Archibald Peabody and ran off what was agreed by all present to be an admirable presentation of the similarities between her assailant and various members of the animal kingdom, starting with domestic mammalian of the lower barnyard and descending in rapid phylogenetic order through rodents, reptiles, and arthropods before finally winding up at several lesser mollusks.

Although Archibald Peabody was not in any condition to grasp the substance of her speech, the tone of Mildred's voice, in conjunction with her countenance, conveyed quite effectively the message that words alone had failed to.

While Mildred collected her littered purchases, Archibald Peabody wobbled off to his car. He returned shortly, bearing with him his cherished implements of honor. One of these he flung at Mildred, while the other, brandishing with a mighty flourish, he ran through his shoe and impaled squarely onto his big toe.

Mildred Contremond was beside herself in anger. She insisted that Archibald Peabody be arrested on the spot.

Archibald Peabody called for his doctor.

Chief Taylor was summoned to resolve the matter. He found, upon his arrival, that the scene had ordered itself into two camps. The one, Contremonders, demanded that he carry the offending reprobate off to the hoosegow without further ado. The other, Peabodians, claimed theirs was the wronged party and clamored for an apology.

While the historian with his dispassionate pen would be likely to concede the dispute to the former on grounds of reason, this estimable creature is never present when most needed, and, as it was Saturday, and Gola's hosting a capacity crowd, the latter carried the day by the more generally successful argument of numbers.

Hoisting their champion upon their shoulders, they marched triumphantly up State Street to Maple, where they deposited him on the doorstep of number seventeen. Luck having been away that day, I was not. The beleaguered chief, after explaining the circumstances of the call, stated that he was leaving the thing entirely up to me. If I declared Archibald Peabody to be in need of treatment, then I could take him off to the hospital and that would be the end of it. If, on the other hand, I thought that the patient required no further medical attention, the chief would request the immediate honor of the gentleman's company at his domicile.

I knew wherein my obligation lay. Archibald Peabody may have made me the laughingstock of town, but he was my patient. That what I had to offer him would certainly prove useless mattered not a whit. Were we to limit our efforts exclusively to those who fulfilled such stringent conditions, our pickings on the vine of affliction would be very slim indeed.

But could it ever occur, in the relationship between a doctor and his patient, that circumstances arise under which the former might allowably disclaim responsibility for the latter? Although Hippocrates had not spoken directly to this question, I felt sure he would have agreed that if, in the course of administering treatment to one patient, the physician runs risk of causing harm to another, then the case becomes rather a different matter. Mildred Contremond was also my patient, and from the look on her face, I had no doubt at all that should I take up the cause of Archibald Peabody, my ability to minister, not only to her, but also to the substantial number of her friends and relations, would be irrevocably damaged.

With a heavy heart but a clear conscience, I told the chief that I considered Archibald Peabody a hopeless case and as such relinquished all authority to that of the long arm. Furthermore, I added to emphasize the point, the man had so ruined his body with drink, that should he continue with his alcoholic ways, it would be not too long before he would be beyond even that reach.

Not too long is one of the two Dumster units of time, the other being *a long time.* Unconstrained by adherence to the more mundane measurements, both are rather flexible in their duration. Accordingly, I felt on fairly solid ground in my prediction. Weeks, months, even several years might pass, but I was confident that eventually I would be vindicated.

The Saturday in question was almost ten years ago. How, has the condemned man fared in the interim? His handsome exterior, unmarked by a single wrinkle, would do justice to one half his age. Every morning he rides ten miles on his favorite horse. Every afternoon he pursues his studies on the battles of the Civil War, upon which subject he is highly respected. His treatise on the battle of Bentonville, for example, is generally acknowledged as the definitive work in the field.

Archibald Peabody Sotwell is, in short, the picture of health. He has, like the wine he imbibes, improved with age. This unfortunate occurrence has given rise in town to the popular reply, when someone employs in conversation the term I applied to Archibald Peabody's demise, as to whether it is Doctor Conger time or Archibald Peabody time.

I have long pondered the question of how Archibald Peabody has managed to elude his just desserts. Having given the matter considerable thought, I have come to a conclusion that, heretical though it may be, is inescapable.

Alcohol has among its attributes that of a preservative. Objects immersed in alcohol, even for hundreds of years show, upon their removal, no signs of decay. I submit that it is this property of alcohol which Archibald Peabody has somehow recruited to his service. By what means he has turned this common poison to such advantage, I am not sure. Perhaps it is in his finding the proper dose—which, as best I can determine is always some, occasionally a lot, never none—thus keeping himself, as opposed to those who drink in an inconstant manner, neatly pickled in a state of homeoalcoholis.

Before I went to Norway, a request from Archibald Peabody for an appointment would have been granted sometime in my next reincarnation. Here he was to see me within the hour. Such is the condition to which I had been reduced.

"Very well, Maggie," I said calmly. "Nine-thirty it is."

Whereupon, in need of my own fortifying libation, I headed to the cafeteria to prepare myself for what was to come.

Chapter 6

Tea

As I sipped my cup of hot and steamy, my spirits were at a low ebb. Perhaps I should I throw in the towel. I was, after all, getting on, and maybe it was time to take down my shingle and make way for the next generation—whose breath was already hot upon my neck. It wasn't as if I had nothing to turn to. I might never be a great writer, but given time, I should be able a least to—

"Mind if I sit down?" came a voice that interrupted my reverie. It was Sarah Trotter.

Under ordinary circumstances, the combination of tea and Sarah Trotter would be just what the doctor ordered for treatment of the sunken spirits. Sarah Trotter was a rock of Gibraltar in a sea of troubled sensitivities. Sarah Trotter was the port of haven in a storm of wounded egos. Sarah Trotter was the perfect pick-me-up for a down doc. Sarah Trotter was a nurse.

Circumstances, however, were anything but ordinary. I gave her an indifferent shrug and stared at my cup.

Some might have interpreted this gesture as a sign that I wished to be left alone, but Sarah knew better. She pulled up a chair and sat down. "Don't you just look like something even the cat wouldn't drag in?" she said cheerily.

I started, spilling my tea in my lap. This was not the kind of sympathetic consolatory line I had expected when I presented her with my best of glum countenances. Had she abandoned me too? Sarah Trotter, who, as head nurse at Emmeline Talbot Memorial Hospital, had been the person most responsible for buoying up my spirits when they were down. No. Others might, but not Sarah. Why then the air of unconcern? I puzzled over this turn of events as I dabbed with a napkin at the tea. Then I remembered.

Several years ago there was a situation in which Sarah had treated me in a similar manner. It involved the case of a patient who came to the hospital with arthritis, and who had, despite brilliant moves on my part, obstinately refused to get better. To be treated in such a reprehensible manner was bad enough, but it was a storm I could have weathered had she not then had the audacity to suggest that perhaps a specialist should be called in.

"I think that's an excellent idea," Sarah had said, a comment that confounded me completely, until she then added, "It would serve her right."

Which it did. The specialist was sent for. She examined the patient and prescribed for her just such a course of action as I knew to be singularly ineffective. The patient, of course, pretended to improve thereby expunging herself from my rolls. Rid of the ungrateful miscreant, my disposition promptly returned to its usual sanguine state. After several years under the specialist's care, the patient died. I do not blame the specialist for this unfortunate outcome, nor do I mention it out of spite. I only bring it up to point out, to those who think the doctor with the specialist's title is the greatest thing since buttered toast, that they might do well to reconsider before they take a bite.

It was obvious that Sarah was now employing that same dash-of-cold-water-in-the-face tactic to snap me out of my present doldrums. Her end I did not question. The means, however, was dubious. To indicate that it had achieved less than its intended effect, I shrugged again and cast my eyes downward.

"My my!" she said, undaunted. "Down at the mouth when we should be happy as a clam. I say—this is a case. This is a case indeed!"

I have never put much stock in the happiness of clams, whose idea of a good time is to spend the day buried in the sand, sucking in water. Sarah, however, could not be expected to know my position on this subject, and so I forgave her the indiscretion. I shrugged once more adding, to reinforce my desire that she shift her current course more along the lines of sympathy, a slight protrusion of the lower lip.

"Well, well. What have we here? I believe it may be—I believe it is—yes, I am sure it is—a pout! Something is seriously amiss. Could it be that the trusty devotees have been a little deficient in the appreciation department? Do we have a few too many thorns in the proverbial bed of roses, eh?"

"Fusswood," I acknowledged weakly, too wounded by this last blow to mount the indignation for which the situation called.

"Yes, even Fusswood." Sarah sounded thoughtful, almost sad it seemed. "Things have changed around here since you left."

"Apparently they have."

"Some things have changed quite a bit."

"So I see."

"And some have not changed at all."

"I guess not."

"Although maybe it would have been better if they had."

"You don't say?"

"I do"

"What for example?"

"You for example."

"Me?"

"For a most definite example."

"Sarah!"

"Sandra."

"What's *she* have to do with this?"

"Everything."

"She does, does she?"

"Yes, she does. For one thing, she's on time. For another, she's not afraid to ask for help. Even from the nurses. If she doesn't know something, she admits it. And she's a darn good doctor. But—that's not it. No, that's not it at all." She paused. "You know what it is?" Sarah punched her finger at me to emphasize the point she was about to make. "I'll tell you what it is. She's a darn good *person*. That's what it is!"

A mathematical genius I am not, but two and two I can still figure. Ten years of dedicated service to Dumster, and this whippersnapper had rendered me obsolete in just three weeks.

I tried to make sense of the rest of what Sarah had told me, but it was no use. My head was throbbing, and I was sick to my stomach. I felt as if I were about to faint.

"I suppose it isn't completely your fault." said Sarah relenting a little. "After all, we haven't trained you very well. What with all the coddling and spoiling you've got—yes, I'll admit it—especially from me, it's a wonder you have any consideration at all. But that's ancient history now. We've all seen the light and we like it a darn sight better than the dark ages. Nobody wants to go back to the way it was, and I mean nobody! Soo—if you want to get back in action, you're just going to have to change your ways, and that is the situation of that!" She folded her arms and looked at me fixedly.

So this was my ration of sympathy for the fix I was in. I was completely beaten down. I looked at Sarah in mute supplication.

"Actually, you don't have to change all that much," she said. Just treat all of us—your patients included—as if we were real people rather than accessories to your own importance. It will be difficult I'm sure, but you might just be able to do it. Anything's possible. You're not all that bad, you know—for a doctor anyway."

And having delivered me this compliment, she addressed me with her crisp nurse smile, she got up from the table and left.

Chapter 7

Retrospective

Like doctors, patients have forty-six chromosomes, opposable thumbs, and can, on a good day, walk on their hind legs. Furthermore, their powers of reason and their capacity for emotional expression are in no respect deficient to ours. In most situations it is virtually impossible to distinguish the doctor from the patient.

But the public arena is a far cry from a doctor's den, and to see in my office the frightened, half-naked soul laid out before me, as a fellow life traveler, is to take a leap greater than my legs are capable of. I am not proud of the fact, but it is True. I simply cannot do it.

It's not my fault.

As it has been decreed in this age of enlightenment, that responsibility for an errant path be ascribed to anyone other than the party of the first part, I would not be acting in discord with common practice were I simply to state my claim to exculpation and leave it at that. This, however, is no common discourse, and I feel it is an obligation to provide an explanation of my confession. Pursuant to this end, I must backtrack to the time of my formative years. Although it will delay the course of the narrative, I think you will find the trip well worthwhile, for it will make clear much that may appear incomprehensible, not only in me, but in those of my colleagues who shared a similar upbringing.

The year is 1964. The place Boston. Our journey begins at the base of Beacon Hill, under the protective custody of which sits the Massachusetts General Hospital. Rich in history, like the city in which it resides, the Mass General can rightly boast to be one of the great institutions of modern medicine.

It was, for example, at the Massachusetts General Hospital that, on October 16, 1846, Doctor William Thomas Green Morton revolutionized the practice of surgery by administering ether anesthesia to Gilbert Abbot in the course of removing a tumor of his jaw. It is telling of the greatness of the hospital that almost before Doctor Morton had left the operating room, word of his miraculous achievement had spread to all corners of the medical world. The surgical amphitheater in which this event took place, now called the Ether Dome, is one of medicine's holiest shrines.

(Equally telling perhaps is it that no mention is ever made of a Georgia physician by the name of Crawford Williamson Long who, on the thirtieth of March, some three years earlier, removed a cyst from the back of one James Venable, having first put him to sleep with that very same substance used by Doctor Morton.)

I could go on indefinitely with praise of the hospital's accomplishments, and gladly would were this the end of our journey, but alas, it is only the beginning. So we leave the MGH and pass along Charles Street to Boston Common. To tarry here on a park bench, watching the passersby and feeding the birds, would be most agreeable, but as we have some distance yet to travel, we must push on. Up the wide expanse of Commonwealth Avenue we go to Gloucester Street, where, turning left, we leave the stately brick of old Boston for the impassive concrete of the Prudential Center. Quickly we cross the Pru and in a few steps reach Massachusetts Avenue and another of Boston's great institutions, Symphony Hall. The strains of an evening Mozart concert waft onto the street. We press onward.

Proceeding south on Massachusetts Avenue, past Columbus, Tremont, and Washington, we plunge into a section of the city populated by litter-strewn vacant lots, abandoned buildings, and a mass of overhead highways. Streetlights gone now, our way is lit by liquor stores. Their flashing neon signs help us pick our way among the derelict patrons sprawled along the adjacent sidewalks. We have turned away from the face of the city and plunged into its armpit.

In the midst of this urban detritus we come upon an architectural monstrosity, a collection of buildings so disparate as to give the impression that the whole lot of them would summarily bolt for South Boston, were they not penned in by a high brick wall that gives the set a more than passing resemblance to a nineteenth century prison. This is our destination. This is Boston City Hospital.

Repressing a shudder, we pass through the iron gates and descend into the subterranean corridors that provide access among the buildings. Narrow and ill lit, the labyrinthine tunnels are treacherous indeed, and someone not familiar with them could easily be lost. I ask you to stay close.

We arrive at a bank of elevators. The sign identifies our location as the Thorndike building. We are met by a man of gargantuan proportions. His huge hands and prognathous jaw give him an appearance more fit for a gargoyle at the gates of hell than the custodian of a place of healing. The giant is called Joe, and to Joe he answers, although whether this is the appellation bestowed upon him by his parents no one, Joe included, has long since had any idea.

Joe greets us with a smile that dispels any anxieties his appearance may have raised. It is a smile comes straight from the heart, unimpeded as it is by having to pass through his brain—this once estimable organ having been rendered almost useless by a rampaging pituitary gland. Joe is an exemplary representative of the Boston City worker, who, in order to keep him off the welfare roles, was placed here along with countless similarly abled employees during the reign of James Michael Curley.

This is hardly the place, we reasonably suppose as we ascend, where healers-to-be would want to launch their careers. And certainly not at all the kind of abode doctors who had made their name at the pinnacle of the profession would want to call home. But reasonability is a vice not much practiced by the profession of which I write, and so it is that among the fruits of the medical tree, Boston City Hospital is considered a plum of the highest quality. Amidst the squalor of the crumbling buildings, happily toiling away, are many of the best minds in medicine. Their pursuits unfettered by consideration of those upon whom they work, they sate their prodigious appetites by feasting at will upon the poor souls who lie within. For although the table may be plain, the fare is sumptuous.

Whatever one might detract from Boston City in other respects, when it comes to patients, it is an institution without equal. Pathology upon pathology upon pathology adorn those who offer themselves up for ministration, and it has been said without exaggeration that a doctor can learn more on one patient at Boston City than on a dozen anywhere else.

We arrive at the third floor and step out into a narrow hallway. At the end is an office. The door is open. We enter.

40

"Doctors," says a rumpled-looking bespectacled man who sits at a desk in the center of the room. "Welcome to Boston City Hospital. Your purpose here is to acquire those two tools which are essential for the practice of medicine, the taking of a patient history and the conduct of a physical examination. These, I am sure, you will master without difficulty." He pauses to peer at us over his wire-rimmed glasses and then blinks rapidly several times before recommencing. "You are fortunate to be here—not, I should say, at Harvard Medical School, for it is Harvard who is fortunate in that respect." More blinks. "Rather you are fortunate to begin your careers at Boston City Hospital," he gestures in the direction of the door through which we have just passed. "A bastion of medical science in a sea of pestilence. A tribute both to the wonders of modern medicine and—" again he pauses, this time removing his glasses and staring at us fixedly, his eyes unblinking, "to its futility. Should you succeed in learning the former, you will become good physicians. The few of you who appreciate the latter may become great ones."

Newly outfitted in our starched white coats, we squirm uneasily and, as years of successful student life have taught us whenever we have not the faintest idea what is being said, nod our heads in vigorous assent.

Doctor Ronald Arky hardly seems the kind of person who will inspire us to the greater heights of medicine. He is clad in a frayed frock coat—once white perhaps but now a kind of amorphous gray, and a shirt of matching color. Hanging from his neck is a heavily stained tie which he has stuck into an opening conveniently provided by the shirt's several missing buttons. He has an unnerving habit of blinking frequently from behind his thick glasses that he looks either above or below but never through, a policy which, given the heavy coating of grime that covers them, is most practical. Seen on the street one might mistake him for some absent-minded clerk who had taken a wrong turn on his way from the bathroom and was trying to find his way back to his assigned station. It is the eyes, however, that give him away. When the blinking stops they shine with an unmistakable gleam. It is the only clue to the burning intelligence that lies behind this otherwise nondescript exterior.

Doctor Arky is a creature of Boston City Hospital, the last in a long line of brilliant misfits who have dedicated their life to the proposition that medicine is a profession the beauty of which lies

41

not in the end of its efforts but in the excellence with which that end is resisted. Eventually, he will become chief of medicine at one of the most respected medical programs in the country—after being evicted from his beloved den by a palace coup that ousted Harvard from Boston City Hospital and sent him across the river to Mt. Auburn Hospital where, although prospering professionally, he has always seemed somewhat out of place.

Having finished his greeting, he pulls from his pocket a set of cards and hands one to each of us. On the card is a name and a location. Our assignment is to find both and return to his office within the allotted two hours. This, he implies, will be more than enough for our first day.

I look at my card. Upon it is written the following.

Muriel Reilly
Peabody 2

Chapter 8
The Ward

"Daahcter!"
"Shut up!"
"Nurrrrse!"
"Shut up!"
"Help me!"
"Shut up!"

Peering through the dull yellow light in the direction of the voices, I could just make out a figure struggling in one of the beds. As I approached the bed, I saw that the figure was covered with some kind of while powder. Upon closer inspection, the powder proved to be snow. It was drifting down from a hole in the window above the bed.

There being no other sign of life on the ward, the exchange I had just overheard was apparently occasioned by my arrival. Absent anything to terminate it, their refrain kept repeating over and over, interrupted occasionally by a convulsive cough from the one or an expletive from the other.

It was, to my student's tender sensibilities, an unnerving scene, and it took me little time to determine that I wanted no part of it. Attempting to beat an expeditious retreat, I backed into one of the beds, producing in so doing, a loud clang that rang about the room. As if on cue, a chorus now arose from this side complementary to that of the other. The resulting cacophony echoed about the tall ceilings of Peabody 2 like the cries of jungle animals in the face of some impending disaster. Desperately I looked about for help. No one was in sight.

My coat! That was the cause of this upset. They had seen the flash of white and mistaken me for some figure of authority. I tore off the offending garment and threw it on the floor. The din subsided. I turned heal and fled for the exit, vowing to myself as I did that never again would I don the garment of which I had just rid myself. It is a vow that, with one disastrous exception, I have kept to this very day. Others may don the cloak with pride. Not I. Many see it as a badge of honor. To me it is a shroud.

My relief, however, was short lived. Hardly had I taken a step when the din revived with increased intensity. I may have been conductor for the overture of this production, but the choir was now performing to its own direction.

My next act I cannot explain. Perhaps it was intuition. Maybe just blind luck. It matters not. Reaching into my bag, provided me courtesy of some drug company making the down payment on what it expected to be a very profitable investment, the letters **Beach Conger M.D.** announcing its bearer in stenciled irony, I grabbed the first object that I came upon and pulled it out. In so doing I loosed my grip on the bag. It dropped to the floor with a loud crash. Twenty-eight heads rose up from their beds. Fifty-six eyes turned upon me. Instinctively I raised my hands to cover my face.

Suddenly all was quiet. Startled, I dropped my arms. The clamor resumed. I lifted my arms again. The effect was miraculous. Peace was immediately restored. I stood there for a moment transfixed. A strange tingling sensation came over me. It was followed by a sense of great warmth. I bent over and picked up my bag. Then I draped the object around my neck and, with a confidence befitting the title I was someday to bear, strode boldly toward my patient's bed.

A doctor must be easily identifiable. This is not hard to understand. If, for example, you were suddenly to drop dead, and a total stranger came up and started pounding on your chest, you would want some reassurance that he was not just acting out his delusion of a gorilla in mating season. Or, if you have been waiting in line several hours to see the latest rage, and some thug barges in without so much as an excuse-me-please, you would want to know that the person is someone to whom you would gladly yield your place.

To many, the outward and visible sign of our trade may seem the coat of white, and once it was. No longer, however. These days everybody from butchers to busboys can be found sporting some variety of the old clean-as-the-driven. No, what makes the doctor is not the cut of his cloth. It is the wave of his wand.

Put a doctor in a suit, and he is Clark Kent. Stick a pair of ears on him, and Superman appears. Clad her in coveralls, and she might pass for a tiller of the fields. Drape the tube around her neck, and her identity is beyond doubt. The stethoscope. It is our sword of Damocles, our Aladdin's lamp, our Samson's hair. Without it we are nothing.

Such has not always been the case. In *ambiance du docteur,* the stethoscope is a relative newcomer. Hippocrates, for example, carried the day without the aid of any such artificial device. Piercing glance, nimble finger, and laying of hand, were the only tools he employed to extract from patients all that he needed to know. It was a modest armamentarium, but for two thousand years it sufficed. Even when it did make its medical debut, the stethoscope's original purpose bore little relation to that which it now serves. The year was 1817. The man, Réné Laennec.

Doctor Laennec was chief of medicine at Necker Hospital in Paris. At the time, Paris was the crown of the medical world, and Necker was the jewel in the crown. Doctor Laennec was a brilliant physician. Patients and doctors alike came from far and wide to partake of his wisdom. In matters digestive, the professor was unbeatable. On topics neurologic, he was without peer. And in covering ground integumentary, Réné was simply astonishing. His knowledge was encyclopedic, his intuition uncanny. Pick an organ, any organ. Bury it as deep as you like. Doctor Laennec could decipher its mysteries without fail.

Well, almost any organ. Like the great Achilles, Doctor Laennec had a flaw. A fatal flaw. His defect, however, was not in the department of orthopedics. It was in the circulation. When it came to matters of the heart, Réné was a flop. At least the matters of one heart in particular. Which particular heart was the one owned by Flossie LaFlamme.

Flossie, it must be said at the outset, was not indifferent to Réné's proclivity to her *situation circulatoire,* but, due to a temporary aberration in French morality, she was unable to requite the love Réné was eager to proffer. With respect to amour, 1817 was not the best of times. Gone were the free-loving days of the Revolution, and gone were the libertine Napoleonics. Staid Louis XVIII sat on the throne. *Egalité,* whose tender shoots had just poked through the hostile monarchical soil, had been crushed underfoot, and form again ruled over substance. For these two flower children, love could not have blossomed at a less propitious time.

The worlds they came from had nothing in common. Réné was a famous physician. Flossie was a cancan girl. Had Réné been content, however, under pretext of urgent house call to steal away occasionally in dead of night, or periodically pack his bags for a convening with his peers at some distant spa, where, as luck might have it, Flossie was engaged in similar repose, none, even if the wiser, would have cared a fig. This would have been readily accepted as a proper dose for the administration of illicit pleasure. But Réné's thirst was too great to be quenched with an occasional sip from the passion cup. Réné needed to drain it daily.

In consequence of his lofty position, Doctor Laennec was attended wherever he went by a horde of devoted followers. It was hardly the life conducive to afternoon dalliances or evening trysts. The obstacles seemed insurmountable.

The good doctor, however, weak as he might have been in judgment, was strong in determination. If he could not get to Flossie, he would bring Flossie to him. Under diagnostic cover of palpitation with a tendency to swoon, he admitted her to Necker Hospital. After repeated and prolonged examinations, Doctor Laennec declared that in his opinion, Miss LaFlamme was afflicted with a rare heart condition which, although it showed no signs of affecting her at present, might do her in at any moment, and she was therefore in need of constant care and supervision by her physician—to wit—himself.

For a time this ruse sufficed, but it was not long before the hours he spent with Flossie ceased to satisfy our ardent suitor, who, though he could gaze upon his love to his heart's content, could do no more. For it happened that those same rules of etiquette that kept Flossie and Réné apart had further decreed that under no circumstances was a male physician to touch any part of the anatomy of his female patients.

Lesser men might have sighed lovelorn sighs. Réné went to work. Sequestering himself in his laboratory, he labored day and night until finally he emerged, bearing with him the device he had designed to resolve their predicament, the *pièce de résistance* that he intended to make his instrument *d'amour.*

The first model was a far cry from its modern counterpart. It consisted of a hollow wooden tube some twelve inches in length with a flanged opening at either end. The doctor placed one end on the chest of his patient, while the other he applied to his ear.

So positioned, Réné and Flossie would sit for hours. He counted her pulse. She did her nails.

Réné, whose amorous needs were comparable to those of most physicians, found that this modest improvement in their relationship fully satisfied his desires. Flossie, however, wanted more. Their inability to use the bed for that which she considered its intended purpose made her restless and irritable.

Sensing that the flame of LaFlamme was cooling, Réné realized that something had to be done. He returned to his laboratory. There he hit upon a simple but brilliant adaptation to his original invention. He replaced the rigid wooden tube with a flexible rubber hose. Now, in order to hold the instrument in place, the physician was required to grasp the distal end in his hand. By this artifice, Réné was able to move his hand at will across his love's heaving bosoms—as well as any other parts within the confines of the instrument's tether, which range, Flossie being quite short and the hose rather long, was substantial. Réné, whose fingers quickly became adept at affording Flossie considerable pleasure, was quite gratified by the results. He was convinced their problem had been solved.

He was wrong. Réné's inventive commitments had forced him to be absent from Flossie's side for prolonged periods, and Flossie, whose love buds were in need of frequent watering, had placed her affections elsewhere. One day Réné arrived at her bedside to find that it was vacant. Flossie had eloped with the porter.

Réné was heartbroken. He discarded his invention and turned to drink. Fortunately for posterity, one of Doctor Laennec's pupils, François Steth, recognized the value of Réné's abandoned love machine. He retrieved it from the dustbin and marketed it to the profession at large.

Doctor Laennec died a broken man. Doctor Steth became rich and famous. As a tribute to his great teacher, Doctor Steth immortalized Réné by naming after him the disease that did him in. Laennec's cirrhosis.

Chapter 9

The Case of the String

Of all the rituals which serve to instill in the neophyte healer the spirit of our great profession, the most important by far is ward rounds. It is on ward rounds that the embryonic physician is introduced to those esoteric mysteries that form the essence of medical theology. It is on ward rounds that the student supplements medical school's meager fare of the science of medicine with the more sumptuous delicacies of its art. It is on ward rounds she learns to think like a doctor. It is there she learns to act like one.

Ward rounds at Boston City Hospital followed immediately upon matins, which was conducted at seven o'clock sharp in his office on Peabody 3 by Doctor Charles Davidson, high priest of the Harvard Medical Service. Matins were a private affair. They were attended only by his chosen prelates, the senior residents. There each resident in turn would offer up to the mentor the lives of the hundred odd souls under their protective wing. He, in return, would pronounce upon each his benediction. Following this, the residents descended to the floors below where they passed on to the novitiates the words of the great master. This was ward rounds.

That Doctor Davidson did not accompany his disciples on their mission was not due to lack of interest on his part. Quite the contrary. He was a kindly sort, and in his own way was genuinely fond of patients. At the time, however, medical canon strictly forbade a doctor of senior rank from the commingling with patients, except in the operating room or the morgue. This was due to concern that such demeaning contact might adulterate the wisdom which had been passed on to him inviolate by the sages who had preceded him. Thus, as we toiled below, Doctor Davidson remained cloistered above, an all-knowing but invisible presence whose inspiration was simply in that we knew he was there.

Having finished my course in physical diagnosis, I had been assigned to a clinical roation on Peabody 1. The senior resident was Wolfgang Grumpacker. Doctor Grumpacker was a huge man, standing well over six feet tall with a wide expanse of bald head and deep set dark eyes that stared out from under a pair of jet-black bushy eyebrows. The first impression he produced upon a person was that he had met up with a not very friendly member of the ursine family. Those who knew him better agreed that both in disposition and in temperament he complemented well this first impression. Dedicated, brilliant, and intolerant of mistake, he was to his superiors a slave and to his charges a tyrant. Doctor Grumpacker was the perfect resident.

The procession worked its way toward the bed of Daniel O'Connor. It would be my responsibility, when we arrived, to present to Doctor Grumpacker the patient's history, my findings on examination, and my opinion as to what should be done with him. On the previous day, I had spent three hours conducting a complete inspection of the poor fellow, grilling him on every detail of his already, at the age of twenty-three, impressive medical career. It included four admissions for broken bones, two for convulsions, three for internal bleeding, five for liver failure, seven for inflammation of the pancreas, and one for a punctured lung. The punctured lung had earned Daniel O'Connor a place of permanent notoriety in the ward annals when, upon seeing Doctor Grumpacker approaching late one evening, he mistook him for a herd of purple elephants. Fearing for his life, he had bolted from his bed, leapt through the window, and fled down the street, intravenous tubing, catheters, chest tube, and all. He made it all the way to Dudley Street Station before he collapsed in an exhausted heap.

"Daniel O'Connor is a single white male," I began, "who comes in with a chief complaint of abdominal pain. He was in his usual state of health until ... "

"His usual state of health?" Doctor Grumpacker growled shutting me off abruptly. "Of the many words one might choose to describe the health of this patient, *usual* is not the first that comes to mind." Pleased with his turn of phrase, Doctor Grumpacker turned to the group and, receiving from them an obedient titter, indicated that he had heard enough of my presentation by addressing his next remark to the patient.

"Well Danny," he said with familiar jocularity. "Still alive I see. Good job. Very good job indeed."

Danny managed a weak smile. He was trying to muster a reply, when he was relieved of this responsibility by Doctor Grumpacker, who suddenly whirled back to me.

"*Doctor* Conger," he said, snarling the title as if it were an epithet. "I do not believe you mentioned in your presentation if the patient was in a state of delirium tremens."

Unable to recall at this point anything I had mentioned, I stammered an unintelligible reply and prayed he would turn his interests elsewhere.

He did not. "Well?" he demanded after several moments of silence on my part.

"Well—"

"You are familiar with the condition, I presume?"

"Uh—yes, sir."

"Excellent. It is reassuring to see that your education has brought you at least to the level of our patients," he gestured to the beds, "any one of whom I am sure would have no difficulty in identifying the condition in question. Tell me then. Does he or does he not have delirium tremens?"

I was confused by the question. The symptoms Danny had related to me had nothing to do with delirium tremens. Furthermore, he had sworn that he hadn't been drunk for over three months. Not that he hadn't tried, he confessed. But every time a drop of alcohol passed his lips it had to make its way past the pancreas, and the hue and cry raised by this battle-scarred organ at the offending substance sent Danny into fits of uncontrollable vomiting. This fact was well known to all parties concerned, including Doctor Grumpacker. Under the circumstances, I thought it best to proceed along the lines of a cautious response.

"I don't—think so, sir."

Something in my answer struck a responsive chord among the others. There was a ripple of suppressed laughter.

"Do you have a hearing problem, Doctor Conger?" asked Dr. Grumpacker with sudden solicitude.

"Uh—No, sir."

"Perhaps then I did not speak clearly?"

"No sir—I mean, yes sir. I mean—"

"I am not interested in what you mean, Doctor Conger," he said dryly. "What I would like to ascertain is whether or not you heard my question."

"I, uh—believe you asked me if Mr. O'Connor was experiencing delirium tremens."

He smiled unpleasantly. "That's good. That's really *very* good! The short term memory, at least, is intact. Shall we try a little further, if that is not too taxing?"

The question, not appearing to demand an answer, I offered none.

"Fine." said Doctor Grumpacker. "Now then, can you tell me if you remember your response to my question?"

"Uh—I said that I—that there were no indications of DT's, sir."

"Aha! The mystery is solved. The misunderstanding, it appears is on my side. Forgive me, *Doctor* Conger. I mistook you for saying that you *thought* the patient did not have DT's. Which, of course, you didn't since, as we all know, doctors are not expected to think, we are expected—" He paused to allow the others, who were now convulsed in merriment, to compose themselves. This he accomplished with one short glance.

"We are expected—?" he repeated, fixing his eyes on me expectantly.

I had not the faintest idea what he was driving at. The best I could offer in reply was a blank stare.

It was not the answer Dr. Grumpacker had in mind. Turning back to the group, he repeated the question and, with a complacent smile, received, in well rehearsed unison, the desired response.

"To know!" they chorused loudly.

"Excellent!" he exclaimed. "Excellent. Excellent. Excellent. Finally we are making some progress here. Now Doctor Conger, I believe you said there were no indications of DT's, did you not?"

"I believe I did sir."

"Yes, you did. And what, pray tell, might those indications be?"

"W-well," I stuttered nervously. "He would have a fever and tachycardia. He would be tremulous—and he would be ha-hallu-hallucinating."

"Yes," he said slowly, "he would. And what *was* his temperature?"

"Ninety-seven point three."

"Pulse?"

"Seventy-six."

"Reflexes?"

"Normal."

"Hallucinations?"

"He didn't appear to have any."

Doctor Grumpacker's expression, which during the course of the above interrogation had been indifferent almost to the point of lackadaisical, like a hound who had just picked up a lost scent, suddenly sharpened.

"Didn't *appear* to?"

"No sir."

"I am not familiar, Doctor Conger, with how one determines the presence of hallucinations by a patient's appearance. Perhaps you could enlighten me."

"Well, sir, what I meant was—"

"I believe we have already dealt with the relevance of meaning here, have we not?" he fired back abruptly. "Good. Now, let us return to the issue at hand which, I believe, relates firstly to the diagnosis of delirium tremens, and secondly to whether the physical signs of said condition are present in said patient," he pointed a finger at Danny, "lying before us on said bed."

"Well, he seemed pretty sensible, when I talked to him."

"Did he? Well now, that's something. It is, at least an observation. *Now* the task before us, is to determine the validity of that observation. Which we shall. You are saying, if I understand correctly, that on the basis of your examination, which, of course, included his orientation, his ability to abstract, his knowledge of current events, *and* his appraisal of visual stimuli, you do not find Mr. O'Connor at this time to be in a delusional state. Am I correct?"

Precisely what state, other than one of total befuddlement, either Daniel O'Connor or I might be in at present was, I must confess, completely beyond my powers to determine.

"I-I-I don't know," I blurted out.

Dr. Grumpacker blackened. A scowl overspread his face. "You—don't—know!" he thundered.

"N-No sir."

"Were I to leave this ward, go out onto Harrison Avenue, approach the first person I met, and ask him whether or not he thought Mr. O'Connor was in delirium tremens, I would be able to get, I expect, precisely the same illuminating response that you have so graciously offered. I had *hoped* for something a little more definitive Unless, of course, after you finish your training here, you are planning to pursue a career in metaphysics."

Now on the verge of tears, I flushed but said nothing. Dr. Grumpacker, having decimated me quite to his satisfaction, proceeded to a dissertation on the concept of uncertainty, which, he declared, might be acceptable for physics and disciplines of its ilk, but which had no place whatsoever in the profession we had chosen.

Although I have forgotten not a word of its content and can assure the reader most positively that were I to relate it here in its entirety, he would find it very enlightening, space, unfortunately, does not permit me that luxury. Suffice it to say that at its conclusion I swore to myself that I would never again utter the three words which had prompted its delivery. In fact, the whole humiliating experience determined me on the spot that henceforth I would always keep an all-knowing upper hand in encounters with my patients. (And it is the strict reliance on precisely this policy that has ever since stood me in excellent stead—until Sandra Smart came along and turned my practice inside out.)

The oration had a dissipating effect on Doctor Grumpacker's wrath. His countenance softened, and an almost benevolent expression came over him. "Now Beach," he said addressing me in a more kindly voice, "perhaps I can help you out of your uncertainty. Tell me if you will, what was the result of the string test?"

"The string test?"

"The string test. You did perform the string test, did you not?"

I had never heard of the string test, but I was not about to repeat my mistake. I had learned my lesson.

"It was, uh—inconclusive," I said.

"Inconclusive?" Doctor Grumpacker leaned forward. His eyebrows arched in readiness for another assault.

"Yes sir," I said quickly. "But perhaps you would be so good as to repeat it for me, sir. I think—er—I have not done the test much, and I may not have performed it properly."

An appreciative murmur arose from the crowd. They knew what I was soon to discover, namely that the tune I had just requested was that which, in Doctor Grumpacker's considerable repertoire, was considered his finest. When it came to the playing of the strings, Doctor Grumpacker was a virtuoso without equal.

Doctor Grumpacker draped his arm over my shoulder in a paternal manner. His eyebrows descended from their elevated position, and around the corners of his mouth there appeared the beginnings of a genuine smile. "Certainly, Beach my boy," he said. "I'd be glad to. It would be my pleasure."

Whose was the better stratagem, I shall not attempt to divine, but it mattered not. He was on the stage. And I was off the hook.

Not so Danny, who, by the terrified look on his face, appeared convinced that the test we had just been discussing involved some form of garroting.

"Well, Danny, my boy," said Doctor Grumpacker amiably, "how is the old pancreas doing today? Better, I hope."

"Uh—not too bad, I guess," said Danny weakly.

"Fine. Now then, there's something I'd like to show you—if you don't mind, of course."

Danny didn't. Doctor Grumpacker reached into his pocket with his right hand. He fumbled about a bit and then withdrew it, his fist closed. Thrusting the fist towards Danny he opened it palm upwards in front of him. Then he brought his left hand into approximation with the right and, pinching both thumbs and index fingers together, slowly drew the two hands apart.

"Tell me, Danny, do you see anything?"

"N—No-o-o-o," answered Danny uncertainly after staring at the space for several seconds.

"Are you sure?" Doctor Grumbacher gazed at him fixedly. "Look carefully now."

Danny hesitated. "Well—maybe. Yes. Yes, I do. *Sure* do! There it is. It's right there, Doc."

"Good!" said Dr. Grumpacker smiling broadly. "Tell me, Danny, *what* do you see?"

Danny squirmed uneasily. "That's hard to say, Doc. I don't see so good any more. I, uh, been thinking I might need glasses."

"Then let me help you." Doctor Grumpacker raised his hands toward the ceiling. "I'll hold it up to the light. Now, can you tell me what it is?"

Drops of perspiration appeared on Danny's brow. "Well, I can't say for sure, but it looks sorta like—uh—you might say it was—more or less—a piece of—" he stopped and looked doubtfully at Doctor Grumpacker, who helpfully unraveled a bit more, "string?"

"Right you are, Danny boy." Doctor Grumpacker clucked happily. "A string it is. That's good. That's *very* good. Now then, can you tell me what *color* is the string?"

Danny was visibly agitated. His hands were shaking, and the sweat was pouring off him in buckets. It was becoming painfully apparent that I had missed the diagnostic boat completely. "Jeez.

That's tough, Doc. You know I'm kinda, uh—color blind. Yeah, that's it. Color blind as a bat. That's me."

"That's okay, Danny. I don't need the exact color. Just give me your best guess. This isn't a test you know."

"Oh." Danny relaxed slightly. "Okay. Well, let's see." He scrunched up his eyes and stared hard for several seconds. "I'd say—but I'm not positive now—that it looks somewhat, on the— uh—brown side." He looked expectantly at Doctor Grumpacker.

"Not bad, Danny," said Dr. Grumpacker nodding in approval. "Not bad at all. But look again. Wouldn't you say, it looks a little green? Especially over at this end." He inclined his head toward his left hand.

Danny applied his attention to the space indicated. "Now that you mention it, Doc, I think you're right. Yup, green it is. No doubt about it. Green as the beer in South Boston on St. Patty's Day—or so I been told." He smiled tentatively at his joke.

"Very good," Danny said Doctor Grumpacker pocketing his string and giving Danny an approving clap on his shoulder. "Very, very good."

He turned to me. "That, Doctor Conger, is a string test as positive as any I have seen. This man is in florid DT's. What he needs is Thorazine, two hundred milligrams every four hours, magnesium sulfate, two cc's, and one hundred milligrams of thiamin IV stat. That should settle him down." And with one nod to indicate he had finished with this case, and a second to accept his accolades, he moved on to the next bed.

It was an impressive performance. Completely taken with it, I forgot my humiliation altogether. I could hardly wait to try out this new found pearl myself. As soon as rounds was finished, I went back to Danny's bed.

"Now, Danny, I'm going to ask you to look—"

"Please, Doc," he protested as I put my hand into my pocket. "Don't make me go through that again."

"But—you did so well with Doctor Grumpacker."

"Uh-huh."

"What do you mean?"

"I didn't."

"Oh yes, you did! You were great. And if you'll just—"

"Doc."

"What Danny?"

"I never saw it."

"You—?"

"Never saw nothing, Doc. Nada. Goose eggs. Zip-po!"

"But you said—"

"I know what I said. I'm telling you I never saw no damn string. Not a bit of it. No way in hell though I was going to tell wolfman. I may be a drunk, but I ain't crazy!"

Chapter 10

On Truth

There are airplanes that travel faster than the speed of sound. There are computers that calculate in less than the blink of an eye. There are satellites that transmit at almost the speed of light. And there are thousands of other inventions testifying to the successes of humanity in its battle against time. But though we can save it, and though we can shrink it, we can't stop it. No matter how great the machine, no matter how mighty the effort, the unmindful clock ticks relentlessly on.

There is one device, however, as old as the ages, and so simple even a child can use it, for which time has no hold. It can take you back thousands of years to any point in history, or forward, if that is your desire, to an exact time and place, whether that place be on the farthest planet in the most remote galaxy or inside the nucleus of an atom on a hair behind the pope's left ear, and it can do this with no more fuss than making out a grocery list. It is the pen.

Having employed this humble instrument for our sojourn in the past, I now return us to the present, to the cafeteria at Emmeline Talbot, where I am meditating upon my tête-à-tête with Sarah Trotter.

It was a pretty stiff blow to suffer in the space of a few minutes, the tumbling down of all the values upon which my entire professional life had depended, and a lesser person might have given up on the spot. However, twenty-five years of fighting the good fight had given me a character of sterner stuff than to quit when the chips were down. The gauntlet had been thrown. Very well. The rules of the game had changed. So be it. Let the games begin. I was ready to play!

At nine-thirty on the dot I entered the office. Maggie uttered a small gasp.

"Fear not Maggie," I said with a reassuring wave. "All is well. Mister Sotwell is ready to see me, I presume."

"Yes, Doctor Conger. He is in your first examining room."

"Thank you. I shall see him immediately."

Archibald Peabody rose to greet me with a grin that bespoke a generous application of his usual preservative. His tongue likewise endowed, he then made an impassioned declaration that included boundless gratitude for past services and a fervent desire that my magnanimous nature would permit bygones to be bygones. I replied with a brief acknowledgment and, salutations dispensed with, proceeded immediately to the business at hand.

"Well, Mister Sotwell. What can I do for you today?"

Sotwell's joviality vanished. Gesticulating agitatedly, he thrust his face at me and exclaimed in a loud voice, "Look!"

Obedience being the new call of duty, I obliged. Absent any more specific instructions from my liege, and without any obvious topographic disruption of the area he had indicated, I made the look a pretty general one.

"Well?"

"Well." I was brimming with my newfound honesty.

"Well—" he demanded, "am I going to die?"

The coupling with taxes notwithstanding, there still remains considerable confusion among the general public on the subject of death. Hardly a day goes by that, upon having pronounced Mr. G. afflicted with p-itis or Ms. S. stricken with m-osis that the first words out of the mouths of G. or S. are precisely those just uttered by Archibald Peabody.

I hasten to add, lest I be accused of prejudice, that this misunderstanding is not limited to patients. Numerous of my colleagues, especially the younger ones, are equally misinformed on the relationship between the death and the practice of medicine.

The Truth of the matter is—and here I must issue a caution to those readers not of strong constitution. What I am about to say may be more than tender sensibilities can bear. You would be well advised to lock them up tight before proceeding further.

If a doctor treats a patient long enough, the patient will die.

To this there are no exceptions. What, you may ask, in the case where the doctor dies? Another will immediately take up the fallen standard. Thus is preserved the sanctity of the rule.

From the dawn of creation until almost the present day, this law has enjoyed a position of universal respect, even among the inferior classes, who, deficient as they might be generally, on the point of consummations devoutly to be wished are fully as appreciative as their betters. In the recent march of progress, however, it has somehow been lost in the shuffle.

In the case of patients, this is not hard to understand. Whereas death once occurred in the home, where it was inescapably in view, now it is sequestered away in the deepest reaches of hospitals, so that one's usual exposure tends to come through reading about it in the papers or seeing it acted out on television. Under such circumstances, it is only natural that people would develop a tendency to place death in the category of things that happen to someone-else-but-not-to-me.

Doctors, one might think, would not be so deceived. Not only are we expected to be in the audience when the grim reaper makes his stage appearance, but not uncommonly we are expected to pull the curtain for him. Such, however, is not the case.

How could this be? Firstly, nowhere in the course of medical education is the principle of the inevitability of death presented to the budding physician. In fact, the entire thrust of medical teaching is directed in an entirely opposite direction. The policy set forth all the way down the line is that if enough tests are done, and enough drugs are given, and enough money is spent, no disease need be terminal. Secondly, people dying in hospitals often do so under unusual circumstances, such as at night, or when the doctor is at a meeting. Usually, the only ones around are nurses, who by nature are secretive. And even if a doctor does arrive at the bedside of one who has just announced his intention to embark for the hereafter, what happens is this: Rather than do the courteous and respectful thing, which would be to say a polite goodbye and wish the departing soul well upon his journey, she will immediately grab hold of it, attempting, however briefly, to detain him, and inflicting upon him in the process such a profusion of tubes and wires as to leave the impression, when the eventual departure is finally effected, that the actual moment of death is some kind of mechanical difficulty, like a burnt fuse or a plugged fuel line, which the doctor, had she just a little more time or some advance notice, could easily have fixed.

Thus it has become the universal expectation of doctors and patients alike that proper medical care will lead, if not to immortality, at least to a reasonable approximation thereof. And the expected response, therefore, to the question which Archibald Peabody had just posed to me, is to reply in the negative.

Which brings up another issue.

When God, in the Garden of Eden, found Adam and Eve admiring the apple of knowledge, he told them that if they ate of it, they would die. This, although technically correct, was completely misleading, as he gave the couple the distinct impression that it was right on the spot they would perish, and not scores of years later from apoplexy or cancer of the prostate. Furthermore, when later on the snake told them the Truth, and they ate the apple anyway and discovered what God had not wanted them to know—and I'm sure he had a good reason for it—namely that what they were wearing was not some type of transparent polyester but his own given skin, God got so angry that he chopped off the snake's legs. Leaving little doubt for future generations as to whether honesty would always be the best policy.

Take the case of the parent and the child. While it is the parent's duty to teach the child always to tell the Truth, the purpose of this maxim is not primarily to encourage the child himself along such lines. The aim rather is to inculcate in the child the unshakeable belief that the parent is an adherent of this philosophy. So that when, in order to protect the child from discovering that the parent might not know what she is doing, the parent must tell the child, not what actually is, but what ought to be, the child will believe the parent.

Likewise is it permissible for a doctor, if she determines that it to be in the patient's best interest, to tell the patient something which, with respect to the Truth, is not strictly accurate. Let me illustrate.

I applied for medical school in 1962. It being the sixties, the people who made decisions about whom to admit were less interested in who we were than in where we were coming from. This they determined by an interview, which was, perforce, group.

There were twenty of us in my group. The interviewer, recognizing that it was a stressful situation, told us that he wanted us to think of the interview as just a friendly chat. He let us know that we had all been carefully selected. All had been excellent students, all had shown outstanding leadership qualities, and all, he was sure, would make excellent physicians. The medical school, he said, would love nothing more than to accept all of us. But the supply of patients being what it was, it could only take one.

"You must understand," he explained, "that what we are about to discuss will cover ground unfamiliar to you. But do not feel that you are unable to answer my questions simply because you do not know the correct answer."

At the time, this comment made no sense to me, and I assumed that it was just one of those things that people in positions of authority say to prove their superiority. As I was later to discover, it is the ground upon which is built any communication from a doctor to a patient.

"Doctors," he said, addressing us in this hypothetical manner to put us in the right frame of mind, "a young woman comes to you because she has found a lump in her breast. You examine her. You determine that it is malignant. You advise her to have a mastectomy. She is reluctant to undergo such a drastic procedure. You explain that it is the best treatment for her illness. She consents to have the operation. The microscopic pathology of the surgical specimen shows the lump to be a fibroadenoma, a completely benign condition. Doctor Jones," he said turning to fellow on his right, "What would you do at this point?"

"I—er— well, I'd call the patient," stammered Jones.

"And what would you tell her?"

"I would tell her—what had happened."

"Doctor Felcher, what is your opinion?"

"My opinion? Is—uh—Yes."

"Yes?"

"Yes, I think—Yes, it would be—yes."

"Yes, you would admit to a patient that you, her doctor, had made a mistake? What do you say to that Doctor Abernathy?"

And so he went around the room until all twenty of us affirmed, with varying degrees of conviction, that we would put aside personal embarrassment and do the proper thing by our patient. When we had finished he looked at us with an expression of the type one reserves for the hopelessly idiotic. He then handed us an article from the *Journal of the American Medical Association,* entitled "Physicians Attitudes Toward Using Deception to Resolve Difficult Ethical Problems." He asked us to read the article and said that when we had done so, we would resume the discussion.

The article described the presentation to a group of doctors of a hypothetical situation in which the doctor is taking care of a very ill patient and inadvertently administers the wrong medication. As a result, the patient dies.

About half of the doctors said they would reveal to the patient's family their error. The other half demurred. As to the latter's justification for their action, they were concerned, they said, not with the effect such a revelation might have on their personal reputation, but—family members being what they are and word of the mishap likely to spread—with the impact it would have on the faith that other patients had in their doctors. Faith, these physicians explained, being the single most important component to the doctor-patient relationship, any act that might jeopardize it, however desirable it might seem from a point of personal integrity, must be shunned at all costs.

"Now," the interviewer asked us when we had reconvened, "what do you think of those doctors who said that they would conceal their mistake?"

Most of us, after a brief struggle with our conscience, conceded the point. A few were uncertain. One—I think she became a lawyer—was outraged.

"Good. Now let me ask you this. What about those doctors who said they would tell the Truth. What do you think of them?"

Several minutes past, but no one spoke. The interviewer looked at us doubtfully, trying to decide whether there was anything to be gained from pressing the case further, and having just about decided it was not, turned suddenly in my direction.

"Doctor Conger?"

I had not indicated any desire to speak, but some involuntary gesture must have betrayed me, for the answer had just struck me with striking clarity. It was something that would have been obvious even to a child.

"It's—nothing, sir." I answered. I did not want my thoughts made public.

"If it's something you think, then it *is* something—*doctor.*" He spoke this last word with an emphasis that gave me reason to believe my response might well determine my fate.

"You want to know what I think about the doctors who said they would tell the Truth?" I ventured, hoping I had misunderstood the question. I had not.

"That is correct."

"Well, sir. I think they were lying."

Chapter 11

To Die or Not

Archibald Peabody stared at me expectantly. Fear showed in his eyes. Every instinct told me what he wanted to hear. Every impulse told me what I ought to say. But I had made a vow, and if honesty was the new policy, then honesty was what Archibald Peabody would get.

"Yes, Archibald," I said, "you will die."

For several seconds there was no visible reaction, and I thought that he had not heard me. This was not the case. In Archibald Peabody's state, sensory transmission lines can be unreliable, and it takes a little time for a message to get through.

When it finally did, the effect was singular. Archibald Peabody's head shot back, his eyes rolled up, and with a spasmodic convulsion, he collapsed on the floor. My prophecy appeared to have brought about its own consummation. I dropped to my knees and was raising my fist to deliver a thump to his chest, when the deceased groaned.

"I knew it," he said. "It's cancer, isn't it?"

I looked at him dumbly. The shock of Archibald Peabody's sudden demise had caused me to forget his present complaint. As I now recollected, it had something to do with his finger. I turned my attention to the part in question.

"Hey!" exclaimed Archibald Peabody abruptly withdrawing his hand from my grasp. "Not there. Here." He pointed in the direction of his right eye. Dutifully I redirected my attention.

The organ in question, other than bloodshot, which, being its usual state, could not be much cause for alarm, appeared normal. Nonetheless, I gave it my best.

"Well?" he asked after I had perused the eye for several minutes.

"Hmmm." I was not yet prepared to commit myself to a more specific opinion.

Archibald Peabody was not satisfied with my offering. "What is it?" he demanded.

I didn't have a clue. This, of course, is the usual situation when doctor and complaint are first introduced, and ordinarily it would not have presented me with great difficulty. I would simply have sent Archibald Peabody off for an assortment of tests, and by the time they were done, either he would have forgotten this complaint in favor of a new one, or something would show up that would allow me to lead him toward a diagnosis more suitable to my abilities. But those were the ways of old, which I had now forsworn. Uncertain how to proceed, I was considering my options when the patient himself unexpectedly came to my rescue.

"There," he exclaimed waving excitedly. "Did you see it?" He pointed again to his eye.

It was hardly more than a flutter, but there it was. On familiar ground now, I advanced easily.

"That's a tic, Archibald."

"I know it's a tic, Doc. I'm no dummy."

"Certainly not."

"Well?"

"Well."

"Well, why do I have it?"

"That's a question I'm afraid I can't answer. I'm a doctor, not a philosopher. Anyway, it's only a tic. Pay no attention to it."

"But it's a sign." he persisted stubbornly. "It must be. Or else it wouldn't be there. A sign of something. I want to know what." Archibald Peabody folded his arms across his chest and stared. He was determined to get something out of me.

Medicine has covered a lot of territory in its quest to unravel the mysteries of the human body, and much progress has been made since the days of the four humors. But there are a few crannies still unplumbed, and the lowly tic occupies one of them. Prior to the taking of my vows, I would have concocted for Archibald Peabody some explanation to reassure him, and it was this course of action that common sense, which had been suffering considerably in the early minutes of this new regime, was now advocating in most urgent tones. The particular explanation didn't really matter, it said. One would do as well as another. All the patient needed was something delivered in an authoritative tone, and he would be entirely placated. If my memory is correct, the one it picked was something along the lines of neuronal instability from an alcohol-induced magnesium deficiency. Common sense, however, had become a *persona* most *non grata*, and I was forced to shut it up summarily.

I knew I was on the edge of a slippery slope, but I had taken the pledge, and I was bound to carry it out. Forcing a reluctant set of lips to form words they had not uttered for twenty-five years, I braced myself for I knew not what, and took the plunge.

"I don't know."

"I knew it," moaned Archibald Peabody. "It *is* cancer!" And burying his head in his hands, he began blubbering like a baby.

"I don't think it's cancer, Archibald," I said.

As I truly did not consider it anything more than a most ordinary tic, this response seemed in keeping with the party line. I hoped it would settle him down.

"But you don't know!" he argues tearfully. "You said so just now. You *don't know!*"

"No, I don't."

"So what are you going to *do?*"

Catscan! screamed common sense, desperately trying to salvage the situation. It was a reasonable suggestion. From a purely diagnostic point of view a catscan would be utterly worthless. Even on the remote possibility that he might have something gnawing away at the ophthalmic division of his fifth nerve, it would be too small for the catscan to find. This, however, did not matter. The test could turn out one of two ways. Normal, in which case I would have a valuable ally in the reassurance case. Or abnormal, and then I had opened up a Pandora's box of possibilities. But I was now on the road less traveled by, where the amenities of misleading tests were not at my disposal. With little confidence in my course, but determination to see it through, I forged ahead.

"Nothing."

"*Nothing?*" Archibald Peabody looked at me incredulously.

"Nothing. The fact is, if you've got cancer, we'll find it eventually, and any test I order is likely to raise more questions than it answers. Besides, if you have a brain tumor, treating it won't make much difference." I was about to explain that treatment might actually make him worse, but stopped. If honesty was the prescription, this dose would have to suffice. I didn't want to overdo it my first time out.

Archibald Peabody looked at me blankly. "Cancer, chancer, shmancer, prancer—" he mumbled, "dancer, wanser, hanser—" Suddenly he stopped and looked up at me, a strange gleam in his eye.

Doc!" he cried grabbing at me violently. "What if it's not cancer? What if it's something else? Something that could be treated. Something like—like AIDS?"

"It's not AIDS." I said. I regretted the words as soon as they were out of my mouth.

"AIDS can affect your nerves."

"That is true, however—"

"So it *could* be AIDS!"

"I have never heard of AIDS presenting as a twitch." It was the best rebuttal I could offer. It wasn't good enough.

"Just because *you* have never heard of it, that doesn't mean I couldn't have it. I could be unusual, you know. *An interesting case.*"

"You are unusual, Archibald. And you are certainly a very interesting case. However, it is not likely that—"

"But it's *possible*. You have to admit that. It is possible." Archibald Peabody was determined not to be consoled.

"Yes. It is possible."

"Well, then?"

I was in a pickle. Promptness, honesty, and respect had gotten me nowhere. There was only one option left on the menu.

"I'm afraid I can't help you, Archibald. Your case is beyond me. I'm going to have to send you to a specialist."

"Not to Hanover?!"

"No, Archibald, not to Hanover."

"So there's someone here who could help me?" he said eagerly. "Like Doctor Smart? That would be great, Doc. I've heard she's crackerjack."

This was actually just the referral I had considered. Sandra was more knowledgeable than I in these new tactics, and maybe she could make them work where I had failed. But there was something in the way Archibald Peabody had anticipated my suggestion that gave me pause. Upon reflection, I decided an alternate course of action would be more judicious.

"I'm not going to send you to Hanover, Archibald, because I am going to send you to Boston."

Archibald Peabody let out a ghastly cry. Then he presented me with an encore of his death scene. This time the wiser, I waited for him to recover.

"There's no hope, is there, Doc?" he said gloomily when once again he found his voice. "You don't have to beat around the bush, Doc. Just tell me the Truth."

For a minute I was too stunned to reply. Truth was what had gotten us into this trouble. A moment's reflection, however, and I realized there was no reason for Archibald Peabody to know that I had been giving him the straight dope all along. It was the last thing in the world he would have expected from me. His reaction was perfectly natural. And for the first time in our interview, it put me on solid ground.

"Yes Archibald. There is hope." Which, as the stuff is always springing up eternal all over the place, I could legitimately offer without betraying my pledge. "In fact I am quite optimistic about your case."

"You mean it might not be so bad after all?"

"No. It might not."

"Then—I might not die?"

There we were again. Back between the rock and the hard place. Was I to condemn him to misery just to satisfy the best policy, or was I to give him what he had come for? Compassion told me to say one thing. Integrity insisted I toe the line. Under the circumstances, I thought it best to waffle.

"That's a difficult question, Archibald. You see, there are certain features of the case which—what I mean is—you see—death—"

Archibald Peabody gasped at my mention of the dread word.

"What I was going to say was that—"

"Yes?" He fixed me with a desperate gaze. It was not a gaze that asked for the Truth. It was a gaze that begged for good news.

"Death—"

"Death what?" he said growing more and more agitated.

Picking my way through this ethical morass, I spoke slowly and methodically. "Death, Archibald—may be inevitable. But that should not concern you. For—and this I swear is true—*all my patients are still alive.*"

"But you said—I mean—Are you sure?" Archibald Peabody was confused by the sudden change in prognosis.

"Quite sure. On further consideration, I find this tic you are so worried to be nothing more than a case of trigeminal spasm. It is caused—it *may* be caused—by excessive use of alcohol. Chuck the booze, and your tic will disappear too."

"You're sure?" He was still uneasy.

"Never surer." Which was true. The tic was most likely a transient phenomenon, and, in the unlikely possibility that it was not, the impossibility of Archibald Peabody's heeding my advice ensured that I would be off the hook on my prediction.

He broke into a huge smile. "That's fantastic, Doc! I—I don't know how I can thank you enough."

"My thanks comes in your continued good health, Archibald. I will see you again in one week. And remember, no alcohol!"

"Quoth the raven," he said joyously. And with the vigor of one half his age, Archibald Peabody Sotwell bounded out the door.

Chapter 12

Cider Vinegar and Clover Honey

There are more difficult ways to make a living than by farming. And there are more difficult places to farm than in Vermont. And if Stanley Contremond had been able to pursue either such opportunity, he would have. But as he could not, he had to content himself with making the most of what was available. Which he did, and pretty well, too.

At the time of his death, old Alfred Contremond possessed, in addition to the general store and his house on Main Street, one hundred acres of farmland along the Connecticut River. In his will, he divided up his property among his four surviving children in a manner he had deemed most fit both for them and for it. To his only daughter Mildred, a dedicated spinster, he left the family home, knowing that of the four she was the only one who had any appreciation of its value. To his oldest son, Daniel, who had managed the store for the last twenty years, he gave the family business. His two younger sons, Samuel and Stanley, each got half of the farm. Samuel, who made no effort to conceal his distaste for country life, sold his share to a developer and moved to Boston, where he went into the upholstery business. Stanley, although he had farmed the land without complaint when it had belonged to his father, also disposed of his share as soon as it came into his possession. With the proceeds he purchased eighty acres of hardscrabble land on the ridge that runs above Stedsville Brook, along with an assortment of dilapidated farm equipment which he acquired at Snide's junkyard. What he did with the rest of the money no one knows, but it must have been a considerable sum, for the riverbottom land was prime agricultural, and the ridge—well, some say that Bill Kenyon actually gave it to Stanley, for he has regularly declared that he was glad to be rid of the taxes, and the entertainment value of watching Stanley try to raise anything on it except rocks was value enough for him.

Stanley Contremond is stubborn. And if he could be said to be truly fond of anything, it would have to be of a hopeless fight. Which, given the battleground Stanley had chosen and the adversary he had picked seemed to be just about the odds he faced. Stanley didn't mind. If he could squeeze out of the reluctant soil each year a few potatoes, a little corn, and enough hay for his score of cows, he was content.

In a good year, Stanley got a slight edge. Sometimes he lost big. But mostly it was a draw. This April, however, nature moved into what appeared to be an irrevocable position of advantage. The proximate cause of this turn of events was a scratch on Stanley's left ankle.

Whether it was the germ warfare waged against the open cut, or the diabetes which Stanley never knew he had because he paid no mind to the fact that for the last two months his already slim body had been steadily melting into a stream of urine, or maybe both, is hard to say. No matter. Stanley treated the wound with his favorite two remedies. Bag Balm and denial. They had always stood him in good stead in the past, and he applied them both in liberal doses. This time they let him down. The cut became a sore, the sore became a fester, and the fester became blood poisoning.

By the time Stanley got to the hospital, he was delirious. He had a temperature of one hundred and four, his leg was swollen to twice its normal size, and there was a huge hole above his ankle oozing black pus. It smelled of putrefaction.

"Stanley," I said after I had examined him, "I'm afraid you're going to lose your leg."

"Thanks for the warning, Doc," he said, clasping his hands tightly about his knee. "I'll keep a close eye on her while I'm here."

How, I don't know, but both Stanley and his leg survived the infection. However, after two months in the hospital, he still had an ulcer the size of the Grand Canyon. I tried everything. Antibiotics, elevations, skin grafts, even a fancy powder that cost ninety dollars an ounce. But whatever I threw in disappeared without a trace. It was like a bottomless pit.

One day Stanley said, "Might as well go home, Doc. 'Spect I can mulch it just as well there as you can here."

I couldn't argue with him. He wasn't getting any better on my time. I told him to be sure to keep it covered and clean. I gave him a large supply of antibiotics, and told him I would check him in a month.

"What for?" asked Stanley. "You been checking every day now, and you ain't scared it away yet."

I told him I just wanted to make sure it didn't get worse, and Stanley said it seemed too bad I didn't have anything better to do with my time. I didn't press the issue. I figured I'd see him soon enough, one way or another.

About two months later I was getting gas at Chet's and I saw Stanley consulting with Armand LeBlanc on a transmission matter involving his ancient John Deere. I asked Stanley would he mind showing me his ulcer. Stanley rolled up his pant leg.

"That's a lovely leg, Stanley," I said. "Now that I've done admiring it, maybe you could show me the one with the sore."

"Can if you want, Doc," he said. "Don't see that it matters though. They's both the same." And he offered up his other leg, which was equally unblemished.

I was flabbergasted. If ever there was an ulcer which showed every intent of settling in for the duration, the one on Stanley's leg was that ulcer.

"Wha—what happened to your ulcer?"

"Healed up, I'd say."

"That I can see. But how?"

"Did it by its ownself."

"You didn't treat it?"

"Sure did, Doc. Treated it fine."

"How?"

"First I took off those god awful dressings. Then set it out on the porch. Figured keeping it holed up hadn't done any good, so why not try a little fresh air. Turned out it wasn't such a bad idea, I'd say."

"That's all—you just set it *on the porch?*"

"Yup."

"What about the medicine?"

"What medicine?"

"The pills I gave you. You did use them, didn't you?"

"Oh *them* medicines! Sure did. Used 'em all up. They worked fine too."

"I suspect that was what did the trick. Sometimes those antibiotics can take a long time to work."

"You can 'spect 'em all you want, Doc, but I'll bet you a day's hay them 'biotics are as innocent of having anything to do with that ulcer as the bats in the barn."

71

"Those were powerful antibiotics, Stanley. I wouldn't be so sure."

"I would."

"Now how can you say that?" I was annoyed at his casual disparagement of my drugs. They *had* saved his life after all.

"'Cause I fed 'em to the chickens. Helped 'em fine, Doc. They been healthy as a horse ever since."

"You didn't do *anything* else?"

"Well—" Stanley grinned a little sheepishly. "I won't lie to you, Doc. I did take a touch of cider vinegar—Like Old Doc Jarvis said. One glass every day. Always use cider vinegar when I'm ailed."

Doctor Jarvis and his cider vinegar treatments had been a staple home remedy in Vermont for the past hundred years. It was hardly the kind of stuff to heal an ulcer, and Stanley knew it.

"C'mon Stanley. You can't fool me. You didn't heal this ulcer with just cider vinegar. You had to use something else."

"Well-l-l—you got me there, Doc. I'll 'fess up. I did."

"Antibiotics."

"Honey."

"Honey?"

"Clover honey. Grandpap used it for all his sores. Said it worked him pretty good. A spoonful a day."

"You put honey in your cider vinegar, and you're trying to tell me that's what cured you. Stanley, I wasn't born yesterday."

Stanley burst into laughter.

"Hell no, Doc. I didn't put it in the vinegar. I put it on the *sore!*"

"On—the ulcer?"

"Didn't put it in my coffee. Course the flies bothered it some at first. I tried to keep 'em off. But it was too much bother. So I just let 'em be. They settled right in. Raised a family right there on my leg. Funny thing 'bout those flies. The ulcer started healing just after I let 'em alone."

"Yes, it is funny, Stanley. Well, the important thing is that you've healed, and I'm glad of it."

"Thanks, Doc. I am too."

Back when there wasn't more to medicine than common sense, people noticed that maggots working on a dead carcass would pick that carcass clean to the bone. Funny thing about maggots though.

They're meat eaters mostly. And they have a voracious appetite. But they're finicky. If the meat is alive, they won't touch it. Put a family of maggots on a sound leg, and they'll crawl around all day without taking so much as a nibble. But give them a nice juicy scab, or a festering sore full of pus, and they'll plunge right in without being asked twice.

Doctors used to use maggots all the time. Maggots U.S.P. Right there in the Pharmacopoeia, just after leeches. Which, by the way, can do as good a job on old blood as maggots do on rotten flesh. With a couple of leeches, and a handful of maggots, there was hardly a sore that couldn't be cured.

But maggots fell out of fashion. With all the advances in medicine, it hardly seemed possible that something so simple and so safe and so—cheap, could do any good. Doctors shunned maggots like the plague. Eventually patients forgot about them too.

Nowadays, if someone went to the doctor and asked for maggots to clean up a sore, she'd probably say, "I suppose you want leeches too?" And if the patient said yes, she'd declare him buggy as an anthill, and pump him full of drugs—and probably some electroshock therapy thrown in for good measure. There really isn't any other option.

People might remember.

Chapter 13
Just Desserts

Archibald Peabody kept his appointment. He also kept his promise. When he returned the following week he was as sober as a parson. And he stayed so. I can't honestly say that he looked any better for it, and those who knew him swore that after two months of sobriety he had aged ten years, but it was nonetheless a therapeutic triumph, and I accepted it as such.

In recompense for our mutual efforts, Providence, the usual purveyor of such successes, granted Archibald Peabody a reprieve from the affliction which had brought us together. His tic disappeared on that day and has not reappeared to the present. This propitious result was further assisted by same Prov, who one day pushed Archibald Peabody off his horse, whereupon he died of a brain hemorrhage.

Archibald Peabody's success notwithstanding, my practice was not exactly thriving, limited as it now was primarily to the stable of Gola's inhabitants, who marched into my office for the Sotwell cure. None of them, I regret to say, achieved the mark attained by their departed leader.

This situation did at least provide me with ample time for my literary pursuits, and were I so inclined, I could have converted my predicament to advantage. The artistic flower, however, doubly struck by a harsh climate and not enough watering had withered on the vine. My urge to write was dead.

I spent a considerable portion of my time hanging about the nurses' station, poking into the operating room, attending meetings, and being more or less a general nuisance. One day at tea Sarah Trotter made a suggestion.

"You should take up a hobby," she said. "Something to pass the time—like building model ships or coin collecting. I think it would be good for you."

It was hardly the most inspiriting advice.

On the whole, I was pretty discouraged by the state of my affairs. The best I can say it is that being on time was not a problem.

It is not difficult to imagine then, how I felt when, upon arriving in the office one morning, I found on my list none other than my former favorite, William Fusswood. I was elated. My patience had been rewarded. The chickens were coming home to roost.

Fusswood quickly disabused me of the notion. His visit, he stated, was necessitated by the absence of Doctor Smart and the recurrence of a problem that he did not feel could wait until her return. Although he graciously conceded that it was good to see me again, he had already sufficiently dampened my enthusiasm for the case, that to be Truthful, I would just as soon have dismissed him on the spot. But beggars being what they are, I did not.

"I hate to bother you, Doc," he apologized, "but as I said, Sandra is away, and she told me if the symptoms came back, I should report pronto. So here I am."

"Those symptoms being?" My tone was frosty. I was in no mood for idle chit-chat.

"That's right," Fusswood said. "I forgot. You don't know about my spells. Funny, isn't it? I mean, time was you knew everything there was to know about me, so I just assumed that—"

"Why don't you tell me about the spells," I said, terminating this unnecessary line of dialogue.

"Right, Doc. This is no time for gabbing. I know how busy you always are, and I feel lucky you could squeeze me in today. What with—"

"The spells, Fusswood."

"The spells. Well, for the past month I've been getting this real dizzy feeling—just smack out of the blue. The room spins, and I see double, and the side of my tongue tingles. It's weird. But it only lasts a couple of minutes. Sandra said she thought they were TIA's. That's short for transient schematic attacks. They're caused when the blood flow to one part of the brain is cut off temporarily—usually from hardening of the arteries. By itself it's not dangerous, but it could lead to a stroke. The way Sandra explained it—"

"I am aware of the condition." The frost had developed a heavy layer of ice.

"Hah, hah," Fusswood laughed easily. "That's a good one, isn't it, Doc. Of course you know what a TIA is. I guess I just forgot myself for a minute. Funny isn't it, how someone—"

"Hilarious."

"Anyway, as I was saying, Sandra said that this TIA could be a sign of some blockage, and—oops—there I go again. It's just hard, you know. She tells me so much about my problems. It's almost as if I were the doctor—but I know I'm not," he said hurriedly, catching my now glacial eye. "Anyway, you know what I mean."

"Precisely. Lie down please, Fusswood. I would like to examine you—*if* you don't object."

"Oh no. Not at all. Hey—you're the doctor."

"Thank you. Now if you don't mind—" I waved to the table. Fusswood complied. I took up my stethoscope and was about to apply it to the side of his neck, when he pushed it gently away and sat up.

"You don't have to examine my carotids, Doc. "They're OK."

"I see. You have had then, I presume, a study of your carotid arteries."

It was an unfair question. While Fusswood had been carrying on, I had perused his chart, and I knew that no such test had been ordered. Under the circumstances, however, I considered my action reasonable. Fusswood, well informed as he might have considered himself, needed some refreshing on who was the professional, and who was the amateur.

"You mean a duplex scan? Oh no. It isn't necessary."

"Not necessary? Not necessary to know if you have a condition which could cause a stoke? Not necessary to know if you have a condition which could be cured by surgery? *Not—ne-ces-sa-ry.* Most interesting, Fusswood. Most interesting indeed—I should have thought—but then you know all about that, of course."

Fusswood was quiet for a minute. "Well," he said, "Sandra *said* my carotids were normal."

"Oh she did, did she? And how did she determine that, pray tell? By intuition? Maybe by consulting with the stars? Or perhaps you meditated upon them together?"

I didn't mean to criticize Sandra, but this whole episode was making me quite upset, and I'm afraid I spoke in anger.

"Don't joke at me Doc—I'm not a dummy you know," Fusswood said firmly but without anger. "Not any more at least. As Sandra explained it, my symptoms were indicative of trouble in my vertebrals," he placed his hand on the back of his neck over the location of the vessel in question, "and that a duplex scan didn't give a good view of the vertebrals. She said they could do an angiogram, but she wouldn't suggest it because I could get a stroke from the test, and surgery on the vertebrals was more likely to cause harm than good."

"I'll admit, it was a little discouraging at first, but she said lots of people have the symptoms for years and never get a stroke. She told me to take one aspirin a day and to let her know if I had any more trouble. So this morning, when I got up out of bed, and I felt kind of woozy—I didn't have any diplopia—that's double vision, but—"

"Fusswood!"

"Sorry, Doc," he grinned sheepishly. "Maybe I better just shut up and let you do the talking."

"An excellent suggestion."

I thought we had pursued this line of discussion long enough. I turned my attention to his symptoms, where I expected to make better progress.

"How are you feeling *right now?*" I asked.

"Perfect. As I said, it lasted only a minute—maybe less."

"And you had no trouble with your vision or your tongue this time?"

"Nope."

The constellation of symptoms, combined with their brief duration, made it very unlikely that Fusswood suffered from anything more serious than a little trouble adjusting his morning blood pressure to the assumption of an upright position. I thought it prudent, however, to intervene. He had, after all, come to see me, and what would be the value of the visit if not to offer him a second opinion—especially one that might be a more substantive in the therapeutic way?

As luck would have it, I had just this morning had my weekly visit with Ralph Pushpill, local representative of MedTex Pharmaceuticals. When it came to drugs, Ralph was my main man. Today he had told me about the wonders of a new drug used for the very condition from which Fusswood had been suffering. It was an unexpected stroke of good fortune. I could show him the old duffer still knew a thing or two.

"This, Fusswood, may be a serious development," I said. Although this remark might be construed as a deviation from the new rule, I thought it permissible on the grounds that I couldn't help him if I didn't have his attention.

Fusswood stared at me wide-eyed. His mouth gaped open. In deference to the new me, I eased up a bit.

"I stress that it *may*. Of course, it may not. As you already know, there is no way of proving the case short of waiting to see what happens."

"But, if I don't do anything—" he broke off, unable to complete the thought.

"I can't say, Fusswood. I honestly can't say. I don't have a crystal ball, you know."

"I know, Doc. But *probably* it would be okay if I waited?"

"Probably."

"*Very* probably?"

"Possibly."

"Oh." His confidence was now completely gone. There is nothing like a little whiff of the old impending doom to take the wind out of one's sails. "And there's nothing to do about it I guess."

"Not necessarily."

"No surgery, I told you!" He clutched his neck protectively.

"Quite right, Fusswood. I am not talking about surgery. I am talking about medication … "

"What medication?"

"It is called Cyclor."

Fusswood fell silent.

"The reports are highly favorable."

"And you recommend it?" He sounded doubtful.

"I do."

"Well—"

It was not a time for indecision. "Only on a trial basis, of course." I said, and quickly taking out my pad, scribbled off a prescription. "Here. Twice a day—with meals."

Fusswood made no move to take the prescription.

"You don't want it?" Despite the snub, I remained calm. "Very well. If you prefer to wait until Doctor Smart returns, that is fine with me. It's just—"

"Just what Doc?" Fusswood looked at me anxiously.

"Well, I would hate to have it on my hands if anything happened to you in the meantime."

"N-o-o," he said slowly. "But—aren't you forgetting something?"

How silly of me! Of course I had forgotten. Completely forgotten. But it was reassuring that Fusswood had not. I went over to the cabinet and took out the samples that Ralph had generously provided me for just such an occasion.

"Here's your starter dose," I said handing them to him. "Enjoy."

"Fusswood did not stir. "That wasn't what I meant, Doc."

The uncertainty shoe was now on the other foot. What did he want? I couldn't figure it out. Fusswood came to my aid.

"What about side effects?"

"Side effects?"

"You told me what it can do for me. Now I want to know what it can do *to* me."

If anyone wonders what has soured the milk of doctor's kindness—why we are abandoning in droves our chosen profession in favor of sheep farming, politics, and other forms of animal husbandry, wonder no more. This is it.

Patients of old were respectful of their doctor's feelings. They were careful not to behave in any manner that might put her off her feed, such as questioning her judgment or failing to respond to her treatments. Patients of old knew that a doctor off her feed would be less likely to drive her shots straight on the mark. Such patients recognized the Truth of the maxim that in the interaction between the doctor and the patient, it was the patient's job to get better, and it was the doctor's job to get the credit.

Today's patient is an entirely different fish. Rejecting any thought of sacrifice, today's patient wants instant gratification for his every need. Today's patient sees his doctor as little more than a body mechanic, a servant, whose sole purpose is to attend to his beck and call and to cater to his slightest whim. Rude, insensitive, and inconsiderate to the extreme, today's patient cares only about himself. Today's patient is a selfish patient.

Take, for example the subject of drugs. There is a lot of talk these days about how bad drugs are. Most of this talk comes from politicians, whom I forgive, because they are accustomed to speaking without having the faintest idea what they are saying. But a lot of it comes from people who should know better. A lot of it comes from patients.

Let me set the record straight. There is no such thing as a bad drug. When something bad happens to a person using drugs, this is usually because the person has not used the drug as he should.

It is unfortunate, but it's not the drug's fault. Even water can kill a person if it is taken improperly.

A person can have a reaction to a drug even though he has taken it as he should. This is a side effect. A side effect is not the drug's fault either. A side effect is just one of those things—like a flat tire or a tornado, that you hope will never happen to you, but if it does, you can't do anything about it—except hope that it doesn't happen again. The proper attitude to have about the whole side effect business is just to stiffen the old upper lip and bear it. None of this whining and complaining. That just leads to a bad attitude toward drugs. That is not good.

Because everybody needs drugs. Even the littlest children, provided it is done under careful supervision. Older children, who sometime take drugs without supervision, can get into trouble. But such experimentation is a small price to pay for insuring that every adult is an experienced drug user.

Sometime in every person's life, there comes a day when something unexpected goes wrong. He races to the medicine cabinet and reaches for the Excedrin. Nothing happens! He drops a couple of grams of C. Zilch. He snorts some Afrin. He rubs in Bag Balm. All is for naught. So he runs to his doctor. The doctor says, "This is a serious case, Mr. Jones. You need strong medicine that only I, your doctor, can prescribe." She dashes off a prescription and sends Jones off with the reassuring words, "This should take care of it."

Which it should, because the first time someone comes in with what seems like imminent demise, it usually is something that would have gone away if the person had just waited a few more days. The doctor, fully cognizant of this, uses her knowledge to ensure that the patient's first prescription experience is a good one.

This is important for the later years, when common sense would tell you to throw in the towel and give up on the whole lot of them, but you hang on, because maybe the next pill will be *the one*. It isn't, but that doesn't signify one bit, because, at the stage of life when things are getting inexorably worse, the hope that they might get better is all that matters.

A patient of old would never ask about side effects. He did not know about such things, of course, but even if he did, he would not have asked, because he knew that a doctor was always acting in his best interests even if a medication she prescribed might, in the short run, make him feel worse. A patient of old had faith in his doctor.

Fusswood was no longer the patient he used to be. Too bad for him. He was digging his own grave. Very well—let him lie in it.

The only problem was that Ralph, being like me a positive thinker, placed considerably more emphasis on the restorative powers of medication than on its negative aspects. He had not mentioned anything about side effects.

"Cyclor appears to be quite safe," I said. "I would recommend the usual precaution of checking a blood count periodically, and of course regular visits, but I think you will find it quite tolerable. Naturally, should any untoward symptoms appear, report them to me immediately."

This seemed generally sound advice for the time being, and it would buy me some time to find out more about my new wonder drug.

Fusswood frowned. After a period of silence, he suddenly brightened.

"Cyclor? Cyclor. Cyclor! Yes, that's it. Isn't the generic name cyclomoperidine aspartate?"

"Uh—I believe it is." Ralph hadn't told me the actual name of the drug, preferring, as usual, to give me the simpler MedTex name, but cyclomoperidine sounded pretty reasonable.

"It's a rather new drug?"

"The latest."

"Hmmm. I think it *was* cyclomoperidine. Quite a remarkable drug isn't it?"

"A veritable firecracker."

"Nothing like it before."

"In a class by itself."

"The effect—"

"Is dramatic."

"So I gather."

"It will make a new man out of you."

Fusswood laughed. "Always joking, aren't you Doc?"

"Pardon?" I said irritatedly. I was not joking at all.

"That business about desquamating interstitial rhambdomyolysis. Is that the kind of new man you want to make me?"

"Wha—uh—excuse me, Fusswood? I'm afraid I didn't quite hear you. What did you say?"

"Desquamating interstitial rhabdomyolysis. DIR. It's some kind of inflammation of the muscles. Very painful I understand, and sometimes fatal. There have been several cases recently in people who have taken cyclomoperidine. Apparently it comes on rather suddenly, and there is almost no warning, except for a rise in the CPK. I assume that's what you were talking about, when you mentioned the blood tests."

"Well, uh—yes. Of course! Among other things I would certainly plan to check that."

This answer, while not quite acknowledging my total ignorance on the subject at hand, was in rough accord with the honesty policy, since the test he indicated was among the myriad that the lab automatically performed on the samples I sent over.

"Yes, the *DAR* is certainly something to be concerned about," I said. "But tell me, Fusswood, how did you hear of it? The condition, I must say, is not widely appreciated."

"From Linda."

"Linda?"

"Linda Wirtheimer."

"I don't believe I know Doctor Wirtheimer. Is she up in Hanover?"

"Oh no! She's on *Too Much Considered.*"

I don't know if any of you live where they have public radio. We have it right here in Dumster. It's down on Main Street next to the old hospital. I know the people who work there. They are pretty regular folk, and when they stick to classical music and nature stories, it's a nice station. But the problem with public radio is the commercials. They don't have any. This leaves a lot of extra air time, and even though the announcers talk real slow, they can't make up the difference. So somebody—and if they tarred and feathered him, it wouldn't bother me—decided that the best way to fill the gap would be with news.

Now when it comes right down to it, there are only two things that happen in the world. Somebody dies. Or there's a meeting. Responsible stations usually cover the whole business in about five minutes. But public radio puts news on the air for four and a half hours every day!

It's not an easy job, but the folks at public radio are a resourceful lot, and they have found a lot of imaginative ways to

82

convert into news stuff that you would assume is ordinarily (a) completely uninteresting or (b) nobody's business. With respect to (a) I could care less. But when it comes to (b) they have done something that is absolutely inexcusable. They have started reading medical journals.

Since they have nothing better to do, they read them hot off the presses. As a result, patients, who also have a fair amount of time on their hands, listen in and find out all this stuff before their doctors, who are too busy trying to save lives to sit by the radio all day. This makes the doctor look pretty dumb—a situation, I hardly need point out, is highly undesirable.

I am sure that if the founding parents had any idea that public radio was going to be invented, they would have written the First Amendment to say that freedom of the press shall not be abridged, except when it interferes with the doctor patient relationship.

"So," I said to Fusswood, "do you want to follow your doctor's advice, or what you hear on the radio." I was by now quite irritated with the whole business and would just as soon have washed my hands of it completely.

Fusswood was unruffled. "Your advice is good, Doc," he said. "And I value it—really I do. But I think I'll pass on cyclomoperidine. For now anyway."

"Suit yourself. It's your body." I was about to add, "And it'll be your stroke," but I refrained. Enough was enough.

"Yeah—Guess I'll take my chances with good old aspirin," he said smiling. "At least I know it's safe. Funny. All this modern stuff, and the best drug for me is aspirin. That says something about something, doesn't it, Doc?"

Ordinarily I am a fairly tolerant person. I can accept almost any amount of abuse from my patients without letting it get to me. I know it comes with the territory. Maybe it was the frustration of trying to cope with this new medicine. Maybe it was the struggle of trying to rebuild my devastated practice. Maybe it was just one of those days, the ones you read about in the paper, where some perfectly normal person goes around town with a ball peen hammer and bashes in the windows of all the automatic teller machines screaming, "I know you're in there Francis, you little rat. Come out where I can see you," and you can only assume that this person's life involved some recent unpleasant experiences with a person named Francis and an automatic teller machine. Anyway, this last remark of Fusswood's got to me, and I snapped.

"Safe?" I cried. "You think aspirin is safe? Come here, Fusswood. I want to show you something. Something your precious Linda Wirtheimer will never tell you about."

The Physician's Desk Reference is a weighty tome in which is contained every drug available to a doctor and every bad thing that can happen with each of them. It is the most highly classified of medical documents. We guard our copies closely lest they fall in the wrong hands. I reached behind me to the bookcase and pulled my copy out. I opened it to the page containing the entry acetylsalicylic acid. I handed it to Fusswood.

Fusswood took the volume and began to read. "Hepatitis, epistaxis, gastritis, ulcers, kidney failure, thrombocytopenia, erythema nodosum ..." On and on he read, growing paler as he went. By the time he had finished, his face had lost all trace of color. Fusswood put the book down and looked at me blankly.

"You mean all these—" he pointed at the page before him.

"Every last one of them."

"But Sandra told me—"

"She told you nothing!" I snorted. "And neither would I, except you've been such a blasted know-it-all. You know what these are?" I thrust the book in his face. "Poisons! Yes—even aspirin—poisons all. Every last one of them! That's what keeps us in business. Even Doctor Smart. She may talk a good game, Fusswood, but deep down inside she's still a doctor! And she knows which side her bread is buttered on. If I were you, you know what I'd do? I'd throw over the whole lot of us—and be glad of it." I slammed the book shut and folded my arms across my chest. Let him try those apples!

Fusswood was too stunned to speak. Although the room was quite warm, he shivered as if overcome by a sudden chill. Slowly he got up from his chair. At the door he turned to me with a look that told me all.

Fusswood had lost his faith.

Chapter 14
Doctor Goodnought

There have been times in my life when I was discouraged. There have been times when I felt sorry for myself. There have even been times when I was depressed. But I never let it get me down. I knew that one has to expect such times if one is a sensitive person. And through it all I was sustained by a conviction. Whether it was the expectation of becoming, or the actual being, doctor has always been my guiding star. Doctor took for me the place usually assigned to religion, which, having been raised as a Low Episcopalian, never provided me with very much in the way of sustenance.

Low Episcopalian, for those not familiar with us, is something God created for a group of His creatures He didn't quite know what to do with. Respectable and earnest, we are well-meaning, but are, unfortunately, unendowed with any capacity for true belief. As we like to make generous contributions to worthy causes, it would not have been prudent to dismiss us out of hand. So our Maker, unable to offer us much in the way of faith, gave us a little prayer book and a large collection plate and turned us loose on the world.

I was, in my youth, a faithful disciple. I stood in the choir—I did not sing, for, liberal as Low Episcopalian standards are on the subject of tone, they could not encompass my extraordinary range. I carried the wafers for our no-fault communion. And I expected dutifully to follow my chosen way until death did us part. But at the age of seventeen, my hormones lead me astray, and I jumped ship for the Presbyterians in my unsuccessful pursuit of Karin Stromberg.

Heresy of this variety, in the time and place of my upbringing, was widely practiced, not only by the Protestants, who have always been pretty flexible when it came to sectarian loyalty, but also by the Catholics and the Jews. It was, in towns like Pleasantville, a time for finding oneself, and our churches subscribed pretty much to a belief in the supremacy of a free market. I do not mean to imply that they were indifferent to their congregations, for they were quite vigorous in the inducements they offered to prospective believers, especially the young, whom they considered a good investment for the future of the faith. Karin, for example, had been recruited from the Lutherans by the Presbyterian Youth Association, which had its own recreation room, a record player, and an excellent collection of 45's. It was a time of great yearning, and my youthful soul, melancholy from unrequited love, was as full then as it has ever been since.

But in the days following this last visit with Fusswood, in my Low Episcopalian soul, a kind of repository for all that stuff whose utility is not immediately apparent, I felt a void. It had not been very full for a long time. Now it was empty.

At night I was plagued by a recurring dream. I am in the mountains. There is a dense fog all around. I am picking my way down a steep path, when a great wind suddenly sweeps the fog away and reveals a giant glacier directly in front of me. So high as almost to blot out the sun, it towers thousands of feet over my head. So deep, it descends into a gulf whose bottom I cannot see. Startled by its appearance, I lose my step and plunge into the gulf. The glacier pulls at me, peeling my skin off like a grape and sucking out my insides until all that is left is my skeleton. Down and down I fall. As I fly past the wall of the glacier, I see encased in the ice, the faces of my patients. I call to them, but they do not answer. I reach out for support, but they have no hands. I never reach the bottom.

It was no better during my waking hours. My work seemed futile. What was the point? Stamp out one disease, another takes its place. Give a treatment, get a complication. It was as inescapable as the falling of Newton's apple. For every good, there was an equal and opposite ill. Usually more than equal.

Each day I came into my office. I saw my patients, and I conducted my business. I did my job. But that's all it was. A job. Gone was the thrill of triumph. Absent the dismay at failure. I listened to complaints. I ordered tests. I dispensed pills. And I thought about the number of hours until the end of the day, the number of days until the end of the week, and the number of weeks until the end of the year. On July 5, 1993, I had a minor celebration. It was my professional equinox. On that date I had worked in Dumster for just as long as I had yet to work before I could retire. I had joined the working class. I was marking time.

One morning I was sitting at my desk with the morning mail. In it was my weekly copy of the *AMA News*. Scanning the front page, my eye was arrested by the picture of familiar looking face. In an instant, I was transported back twenty-two years.

It was the winter of 1972. I had just finished my first year at the Center For Disease Control in Atlanta as an officer in the Epidemic Intelligence Service—one of the government's super spies in the war against communicable diseases. It was exciting work, and I was convinced that this was where my future lay. Others could waste their time with bandaid medicine. My call was with the greater glory of disease prevention. Smallpox, polio, and measles were dragons already slain or dying. Still to be conquered were influenza, meningitis, and legionella. We were a dedicated band of warriors, our zeal aided considerably in the knowledge that should we stumble, there were hundreds of others eager to take our place. For this was a time when doctors who could not find accommodations in the service of their country at home, were offered the opportunity to try their hand in Vietnam. Our official title notwithstanding, among the other branches of the uniformed services, we were known as the yellow berets.

On temporary leave from the battlefield, I was driving with my family to the Okefenokee Swamp for a weekend holiday. We had stopped for supper at a roadside park on the edge of the swamp. While we were preparing our food, a bear wandered into the clearing. There was much anxiety among the other family members upon his appearance, and proposals for immediate departure arose on all sides. Desirous of proving that their fear was unjustified, I approached the bear, who, I had already ascertained, was but a cub. I offered him a hot dog. He eagerly accepted it.

It was a perfect lesson for the children, showing them that creatures of nature and creatures of man can live peacefully together in mutually supportive harmony. Perfect that is except for two minor details. The first was that the cub, not being accustomed to the proper etiquette in consumption of wieners, mistook my hand for the bun. The second was that just as I had begun feeding him, his mother arrived and proceeded to indicate, in no uncertain terms, her displeasure that her child was not only eating between meals, but accepting food from a stranger to boot. Bowing to her maternal authority, I quickly conceded the point, and, with the briefest of apologies for my indiscretion, left parent and child to their own devices. In my haste to quit the scene, I tripped over a log.

My wife, after a few comments on the lesson I had just presented, packed me, my bloodied hand, and my swollen ankle into the car and sped off in search of the nearest medical facility. The first town we came to was a place called Council Flats. We were in luck. Council Flats had a doctor. The man at the gas station told how to find his office.

"**Joseph Goodnought MD. Hours—Whenever**," read the sign. Below was a button with an additional sign, "**Ring me**." I rang. Presently the door opened and a cheerful looking bespectacled man of about thirty appeared.

He looked briefly at my bloodied hand "Ah. Been feeding the bears, have you?" he said. "Come on in."

We entered through the kitchen. A large pot of stew simmered on the stove, and from the oven came an aroma of biscuits. He directed the rest of the family to help themselves to supper, which, as our own meal had been prematurely terminated, they readily obliged. Then he beckoned me to accompany him to his office in the back of the house.

Initially I had considered it advisable to tell him that I was a fellow practitioner. This, I thought, would help him better to treat me. I had prepared an explanation for the circumstances occasioning my wound, one that involved fixing a flat tire and a slipped jack. This was not due to any embarrassment on my part relative to its actual cause. I simply did not want to create undue anxiety in town that there might be a vicious bear on the loose. Something about his greeting, however, made me rethink these strategies. I decided instead that silence on both parts would be the best policy.

After forty-five minutes he had put my hand back together. It was as fine a piece of needlework as I had ever seen. He then turned his attention to my ankle.

"Looks like a sprain," he said after examining it. "We'll ice it for about an hour, and if you keep off it for the next couple of days, it should be OK. If it isn't get better by Tuesday, you probably ought to see somebody who's smarter about bones than I am."

"Shouldn't you take an x-ray?" I said. I was not particularly impressed at his cavalier treatment of my grapefruit sized ankle. "How can you be sure it isn't broken?"

"Can't," he conceded cheerfully. "It's just a guess."

"A guess?" I exclaimed angrily. If this was his idea of humor, I did not find it amusing.

"Yup. That's what I do mostly. Usually they turn out OK. Like right now I'd guess you don't have a heart attack—or appendicitis either. But if you want to know for sure, I can send you over to Valdosta. You can get an x-ray of your ankle there, and, if you want, an electrocardiogram and an appendectomy too."

Valdosta was an hour and a half away. I took the guess.

"I'm going to make another guess." He felt my pulse and pulled back my eyelids. "You lost more than a battle out there. Looks to me you're a pint or two short of a full tank."

Suddenly I felt very faint. "Maybe I *should* go to the hospital. They could check my blood count too."

"Suit yourself," he said calmly. "But I'd say you're not in any great shape to travel right now, and my guess is you'll do just fine if you lay low for tonight—assuming that is, we aren't attacked by bears."

"Is there someplace in town we can stay?" Despite myself I was feeling a little better. Something about his manner was reassuring. If he wasn't worried, I guess I needn't be. After all, he *was* the doctor.

"Sure is. It's not fancy, but it's clean, and the service ain't bad."

"I'm sure it will be fine." I was greatly relieved not to be spending the night in our tent. "How do we get there?"

"Easy. Go back to the kitchen. Just past the stove take your first right. You can't miss it. There's a double bed and two cots."

I said we couldn't think of it, putting him out like that, and on a Saturday night. But my protestations were useless. There really wasn't any choice, he explained. Council Flats didn't have a motel. "Anyway, that's what the room is for," he added. "It's part of the facilities."

Many of his patients traveled a considerable distance to see him, and after having a fracture set or a wound sutured, they sometimes didn't feel up to the long trip home. "Council Flats General Hospital. I call it." he said his eyes twinkling good-naturedly. "Don't know if it's up to accreditation standards, but nobody's ever died here." He rapped twice on his forehead to emphasize the point.

He led me back to the kitchen, where the rest of the family was hard at work on the stew. I didn't feel much like eating, so I sipped on some broth while the others ate. Afterwards, a warm fire and the loss of blood, conspired against me, and I went straight to bed.

In the morning he greeted us with a hearty south Georgia breakfast—grits, sausage, fried eggs, and a great mound of hash browns—the whole lot swimming in a sea of sorghum molasses.

I looked at the meal doubtfully. "You've lost more than blood," he said firmly as he pushed the food at me. "Eat up. You look like you haven't had a decent meal in months, and I'd guess there isn't enough cholesterol in you right now to whistle a jig."

He was right. Ever since my father died of his heart attack, my diet had looked like something out of *The Finicky Rabbit's Cookbook*. I took one look at the forbidden fare and plunged in. In my weakened condition, it was too good to resist. Besides, I was only following doctor's orders.

"Take your time with breakfast," he said. "I've got some house calls to make and probably won't be back till afternoon. Just close the door when you leave and don't worry about the dishes. It comes with the room and board."

"What about the bill?" I was surprised that no mention had been made of one.

"The bill?" he said absently. "Oh yes." He paused for a moment and eyed us critically, like a prospective buyer at auction assessing some choice head of livestock. "I'd guess you folks look reasonably prosperous—professionals probably. Both of you? Thought so. That's too bad." He shook his head. "You see, I reckon by the accounting method of R. Hood. I'm afraid I'll have to charge you top rate."

"So—let's see." He took up a pencil and a scrap of paper. "Examination, minor surgery, medications, overnight observation, tax—"

"Tax?" I interrupted. I had never heard of a tax on medical services. It sounded to me more like bill padding.

"Clinch County Health and Welfare Fund. I'm the tax collector. Helps to pay for the ones who don't have anything." He consulted again with his pencil. Having finished, wrote down a figure on a piece of paper. "Think that's about city prices," he said passing it to me.

I looked at the bill. It was substantial, but fair. "Good guess."

"Like I said, I'm a good guesser."

We all thanked him profusely, and I told him I couldn't begin to express how much I appreciated the treatment he had given me. He said he was sure I couldn't, but the next time I heard somebody putting down country doctors, maybe I could put in a good word for them. I said I certainly would. He headed out on his house calls. We prepared to embark for home.

All the way back to Atlanta I thought about Doctor Goodnought. I had never met anyone like him. He was a competent doctor, of that there was no doubt. But competent doctors are a dime a dozen. The thing that I couldn't get over, the thing that all of us kept saying over and over to each other—he was so *nice!* A doctor who was a nice. It just didn't seem possible. By the time we reached home, I had made up my mind. I was going to follow in his footsteps. I would become a country doctor.

When I was done with my tour of duty at the CDC, I made a pilgrimage to California. There, immersing myself in the urban underserved, I worked in San Francisco, tending to drug addicts, alcoholics, and the homeless, whose medical services, if not so geographically distant as in the country, were at least equally inaccessible.

After eight years, blessed with a generous infusion of Berkeley and the guidance of a new wife, I felt ready to make the move. In July of 1982, the dream became a reality. We arrived in Dumster. Here I planned to spend the rest of my days, healing the sick, splitting wood, and being generally adored by the people around me.

In recent years, time and memory being what it is, I hadn't thought much about Doctor Goodnought. But there he was, smack in the middle of the front page, staring out at me with that same friendly face I now remembered so well. Wondering what honor had landed him this recognition, I scanned the page for the accompanying story.

NABBED BY FEDS: FBI agents last week arrested Joseph Goodnought, former vacuum cleaner salesman and self-styled general practitioner, who, despite having no more formal education than a high school diploma and a certificate from the Hoover Institute of Home Cleaning, had successfully passed himself off for the last twenty-six years as a physician in the small south Georgia town of Council Flats. Diligent police work had lead to the discovery of his fraudulent practice ably assisted by the Georgia State Medical Society, which, upon receiving a complaint from one of his patients, discovered that no one by that name was licensed to practice in the State of Georgia. "This is the kind of person who gives medicine a bad name," said C. Henry Turnbull, president of the Georgia State Medical Society. "Who knows how many people this bum may have killed. They should lock him up and throw away the key."

The story did not contain any details of the complaint, but it implied it had to do with the prescription of narcotics. It went on to speculate how Doctor Goodnought had managed to avoid detection for so many years and ended with the statement, "Ironically, virtually every one of Council Flats' eleven hundred citizens has come to the defense of Doctor Goodnought. They had presented the state with a petition urging it to grant him an honorary license so he could continue to practice. It just goes to show how cleverly a charlatan can deceive his victims."

A flood of emotions rushed confusedly through me. Anger, hurt, sorrow, bitterness. I couldn't make sense of it. My idol was fallen. The man whose footsteps I followed had feet of clay.

Following so closely on the heels of my encounter with Fusswood, this setback was too much for my wounded sensibilities. Too distraught even to show up at the office, I moped around the house all the day long. I made some feeble excuse to Maggie about the flu that, given the anemic activity of my practice, she readily accepted. By the end of the week, it was clear that I was in no mere funk. Plagued with doubt, inadequacy, and a host of other emotions that I thought had been banished forever when I took the Hippocratic Oath, I felt vulnerable and unsure of myself.

I felt human.

"Why don't you go see him?" asked Trine. "The only way you're going to get this monkey off your back is to confront it."

It was a sensible suggestion. I had thought about writing, but she was right. I had to meet him face to face. So I hopped a plane to Atlanta and, stopping just long enough to pick up a rented car, drove out to Council Flats.

"Well, well, if it isn't old Bear Feeder," he said greeting me at the door. In his hand was a smoldering pipe and under his arm a rolled up magazine. Except that he was a little grayer on the sides and a little thinner on top, he looked not a whit different from our first meeting some score of years ago.

"Come on in. The stew is cold, but the chair's warm, and so is the whiskey." He gestured to one of a pair of old leather chairs in the living room between which sat a bottle of liquor and a glass. "Pull up your feet and unload your brain. From the looks of you I'd guess both of them have been working overtime lately."

"You B-b-b-blackguard," I spluttered, unable to bring myself to utter the word I had wanted to say. "So many people. So many years! So much—Look at that!" I screamed pointing to the copy of *New England Journal of Medicine* he held in his hand. "How can you? How dare you? How—" Too agitated to speak, I just stood there and shivered with rage.

"A little sensitive today aren't we, Doc?" he said calmly, betraying not the least sign of perturbation at my outburst. "Could it be a little too much righteous indignation—or perhaps not quite enough Lithium?" He paused to consider the question. "The former, I'd guess—although there are definite features of hypomania. But you didn't come here for a diagnosis, did you? No. Well then. You might as well sit down and have it out with me. Lord knows everybody else has." And so saying, he hoisted his glass and nodded at me with a not unfriendly wink. "Cheers. To Hippocrates. To Galen. To Cushing. And to—Conger was it? Yes, I thought so. Mighty healers all. Salutations from and humble forgiveness for your unworthy servant, Goodnought." Concluding his toast, he bowed deeply and sank back into his chair.

"How did you know I was a doctor?" I was thoroughly disconcerted. Evasion, contrition, even indignation I could have dealt with, but not this self-effacing jocularity. There was something in what he said that made me feel as if it were I rather than he who was in the wrong.

"Just a guess," he said laughing at my discomfiture. "How do you know a bear? It's got a nasty growl, and it bites the hand that feeds it. Besides, the only visitors I get from out of town are nosy reporters and outraged doctors. Since you're not one of the former, then you must be—anyway, you want to know how I did it, right? Okay—pull up a chair and let kindly old undoc good-for-nought tell you his life story." There was no bitterness in his voice as he spoke, only that relentless good humor as he began the story of his career as a general practitioner without portfolio.

"I was living in north Florida in the mid-sixties, selling vacuum cleaners. It wasn't a great job, but I was making a decent living. Always have been pretty good at selling."

"Evidently."

"One day I saw this story in the paper about a town in Georgia that had been trying to get a doctor for five years without any luck. I said to myself, I wonder if a fellow could get away with it—passing himself off as a doctor in a small town like that, where nobody would be likely to look too closely at the papers on the wall. The more I got to thinking about it, the more the idea took hold of me. I don't know why. It was just one of those things. You know, like Mount Everest. Because it was there. So I decided to pay the town a visit. Just to look around, I said. I bought myself a bunch of medical books. I got a long white coat with Joseph Goodnought M.D. stenciled on the pocket and a gold plated rubber hose, and off I went. Never thought I was serious about it. Just a lark I figured. Anyway, when I arrived in town and hung up my shingle, the reception I got would have pleased the pope. I'll admit, it went to my head. 'Why not,' I said. Play the game for a few months and then move on. Can't do any harm I figured."

"How could you be sure?"

"I couldn't. And at first I was terrified about missing a serious problem. But I found out pretty quick that most of medicine, at least my kind, was a little common sense and a lot of listening. If someone looked really sick, I sent them to Valdosta."

"At the end of the second month, I started giving hints that I might pull up stakes, but the folks raised such a fuss I decided to stay a little longer. Pretty soon I forgot about leaving. By the end of the first year, I had pretty much forgotten about the missing degree too."

"But you didn't know any medicine."

"Wrong-o, pill pusher. What I didn't know was medical school, which, I'd guess, is about as useful out in the trenches as a diploma from the College of Taxidermy."

"I studied the Merck Manual and Goodman and Gilman's Pharmacology cover to cover and back again. I subscribed to medical journals. I got a mess of pigs feet—to practiced my surgical skills on. And whenever I sent a patient to a specialist, I called him up to talk over the case. I even went to a medical meeting. Once. That was enough. It was quite an eye opener. Most of the doctors there didn't know any more than I did, and they all cared more about the their practice as a business than the business of their practice.

"But you know what helped me the most? My patients. First thing after they had told me their story, I'd say, `Mr. Jones, this case of yours is a pretty tough one. I'm going to need some expert help here. Tell me, what do you think is going on?' It got to be a standard joke around town—Don't go to Doc Goodnought unless you know what's wrong. You know, it's amazing what they pick up. And the patients loved it. Made them feel we were working on the problem together—But I'm not telling you anything you don't know. How long you been in this business?"

"Uh—Twenty-six years."

"Let's see." he said. "That means you graduated from medical school in—1967. Right? That's the same year I moved to Council Flats. Guess you could say we're sorta classmates. I started off a little behind, but I'd guess I'm pretty well caught up now—although it still helps me to stick with the rules I made up when I didn't know any more than a tadpole in a mud puddle.

"Rules?"

"Goody's Goldies I call them. They helped me out of a lot of jams back then. Still do too."

"Er—What are they?" I was unable to contain my curiosity about how this charlatan had managed to succeed for so long.

"Nothing fancy. Just common sense mainly."

"I mean—"

"Ohh—" he said grinning broadly. "I forgot. They don't teach you guys that kind of stuff do they? So you want to know the actual rules. OK. There's just four of them."

"Rule number one," he ticked off his thumb. "If a patient doesn't feel better, he isn't better."

"Rule number two," he raised his index finger. "When you don't know what's going on, say so."

"Rule number three. Never order a test if you don't know what to do with the results.

"Rule number four. Avoid drugs."

The words had a familiar ring to them. Still, something puzzled me. "I thought it was a narcotics prescription that got you in trouble." I said.

"It was. A guy from New York came in one day. Passing through on his way to Cape Kennedy. Some big shot executive type. Said he had a bad back and needed Percodan. Even had a letter from his doctor back home saying he was on the up-and-up. I told him no dice. He got all in a huff and reported me to the medical society. Come to find out the fellow was addicted to the stuff. He had stopped at some fifteen doctors on his way south. Every one of them had given him a hefty supply. But that didn't help me any."

"So one of your own rules did you in."

"Yeah. Funny isn't it. You know, for a while I actually thought they might let me go with a slap on the wrist. You know, young man with no formal education lifts himself up by his bootstraps. Hah! You would have thought I was a mass murderer the way they came down on me.

"This man is a threat to the foundations of medicine." said old Turnbull. Guess he was right though, especially if that foundation depends on high fees, useless tests, and toxic drugs. If I were more sensitive, I suppose I'd get upset. I'm a damn good doctor, medical school or not. But hey, I've had a good time here. I can't kick."

"What are you going to do now?" I asked. Despite myself I was feeling a little sorry for him.

He shrugged. "Nothing special. Hang around here. Mow the lawn. Go fishing."

"But, after all this—I mean the charges and the publicity—aren't the people—"

"Behind me one hundred and ten percent. Actually, I think it's going to be okay. My lawyer is working out a deal with the vultures from Atlanta. All they really care about is making sure I don't practice medicine, by which they mean collect fees. If I do community service, they're willing to forego a jail sentence. As it turns out, there's a perfect opportunity for me do just that."

"In Council Flats?"

"Hey, not a bad guess," he said laughing. "You see, it just so happens that right after this whole fuss broke out, the Council Flats voted to have its own health officer. They were tired of depending on someone from the county. Never could get him when you needed him. I said I'd be willing to take the job. The state said it was okay with them if it was okay with the town—which it was. Now Council Flats is not a rich town, but folks here worry a lot about their health, so they made it a full time job."

"Full time?"

"You'd be surprised how much there is to do, even in a small town like Council Flats. I keep an eye peeled for smallpox and malaria, and I sniff around for leaking sewage. Then there's rabid animals to check out. A lot of stuff like that."

"That isn't—"

"Of course, my duties are a little more extensive than your basic town health officer.

"But surely you don't try to practice medicine!" I exclaimed. It seemed as if that was exactly what he intended to do.

"Heaven forbid. After all, I'm no doctor. But I can give advice. If someone comes to me with what looks like pneumonia, I can tell them. And there's no law against saying a touch of penicillin might be in order."

"What good does that do? If someone has pneumonia, he needs more than advice."

"Right you are, Doc. But the folks seem to like it. Funny thing," he said. "I was talking to the guy who runs the feed store the other day. You know what he told me? Ever since they shut down my practice, his veterinary medicine business has been booming. People are coming in all the time for the stuff. People he's never seen before. People he didn't even know had animals. Must be some kind of epidemic going on. I'm looking into it now. I'm wondering if the animals are getting sick from the people. Wouldn't that be something?"

"Why—What you're doing is—"

"Shhh?" he whispered, winking at me with a conspiratorial grin. "Not so loud. You know what would happen to me if these folks found out that what we have here is socialized medicine in a town health officer uniform? They'd lynch me! I love them dearly, but when it comes to politics, Council Flats is a little to the right of Attila the Hun." He broke into a fit of laughter that prevented him from speaking for several minutes.

"So-o-o—" he said when he had recovered. "What do you think of old quack-quack now? Am I a bum, or am I a bum?" he smiled broadly and spread his arms wide.

I felt the almost invisible scar on my right hand. I thought about what he had said. Medical school or not, he was right. And it was probably because of the *or not* rather than in spite of it.

"I think you're the best damn doctor I've ever met," I said without hesitation. "I think I'd like to shake your hand. And then I think I'd like to take you out to dinner."

"At least I don't bite," he said sticking out his hand. "I'll take the shake, but I'm going to pass on the bake. It's Sunday. I've got house calls to make.

Chapter 15

New Prospects

My visit with Doctor Goodnought had the salutary effect of dispelling the pall that had clouded my days. To see someone who had been through what he had still retain his enthusiasm for the practice of medicine was enough to make even my sensitive soul reconsider its plight. And so it was that I found myself, upon my return, quickly back in the thick of things, and a modest but steady stable of new patients was sufficient to resurrect my usually optimistic temperament.

I must say, as we will not be meeting up with him again for some time, and I wish to put the reader at ease about his condition, that Fusswood has also recovered fully from the great breach. I saw Sandra shortly after her return, and she mentioned that Fusswood had checked in with her. He was feeling fine, she said, but had expressed concern that I had seemed rather out of sorts when he had visited me.

It was not, however, the same Doctor Conger who again took up pad and stethoscope to fight the good fight. True, to external appearances I had not changed. And to my patients I am sure I seemed the same kindly-old whom they thought they knew so well. But I was not. Like a tightrope walker who has taken a bad fall, or the gambler whose lucky number has failed him, the events of the past few months had taken their toll on my confidence. I could still glean from my patients a respectable diagnosis, and I could provide them with a reasonable treatment, but my offerings were uninspired. Gone was the flair that comes when a doctor practices his trade with the reckless abandon of one who can do no wrong. And gone with it, as inevitably as night follows day, was that magical ability to heal by inspiration. If a patient got better, it was likely because he was bound to anyway, and if the medicine I had given him proved beneficial, the effect was probably due more to the contents of the pill than to the urgings of the pill pusher.

It was on this last point that my diminished store of wizardry was most severely taxed. For it is in this arena that the doctor at the peak of his game can most amplify the good and minimize the ill of those he treats.

"Why don't you try this one?" I would say when handing out a prescription. "It might help. But—maybe it won't. And, of course, it could make you sick. But maybe it won't. It isn't great, but it's the best we've got."

Needless to say, this soft sell did not do wonders for my cure rate. Fortunately, this was not of much concern to the patients who now constituted my practice. As a group they had pretty low expectations, and they were usually satisfied if they survived our encounters without serious bodily harm.

I was in my office one day, meditating upon this turn of events, when Doctor Hurbalife dropped in. We got to chatting, and I told him about the episode with Fusswood.

"Beach my boy," he said throwing his arm around my shoulder in a paternal kind of way. He didn't mean any disrespect. It was a habit of his, left over from his professorial days. "What else could you expect from her?

"Sandra?" I asked. "No. It's not her fault."

"Science."

"Science?"

"Science. *Noble* science. *Fair* science. Hah! Fair indeed! Science, my friend, is a lady not to be trusted. Give her your hand, and she'll lead you astray. Give her your heart, and she'll break it. Stay away from her. She is to be avoided. Avoided at all costs." Concluding this remarkable pronouncement, he folded his hands and looked at me with the air of one who had made a declaration, the finality of which was beyond dispute.

As I have already mentioned, Doctor Hurbalife, although once one of the great men of contemporary medicine, was now a few cards short of canasta. But he was a friendly sort, and I was in need of company, so I humored him.

"Enlighten me, Doctor H.," I said. "I'm all ears."

He was delighted at the chance to expound upon a favorite topic.

"Since the days of Galileo, it has been the role of science to explain the inexplicable, to justify the unjustifiable, and to scrutinize the inscrutable. It has been science's forthright and, I must say, perverse pleasure to take out of life the one thing in it which is truly worthy of preserving—to wit, its mystery.

"Now there can be no denying that she has produced, in the course of her labors, numerous material benefits. These, I will concede, have made life a more convenient business. However, taken on the whole, I think we can fairly say that the intrusion of science into the life of man has been an utter disaster, and nowhere is the proof of that point more evident than in that very profession we call our own—which profession, I hardly need emphasize, has been quite stolen out from under us by this bewitching vixen."

"How so?"

Although I had not the faintest idea what he was driving at, his speech had tweaked my curiosity.

Doctor Hurbalife screwed up his eyes tightly simultaneously pursing and unpursing his lips several times in rapid succession. Then, placing his hands on either side of his nose, he rubbed them briskly back and forth until the nose almost glowed from the effort. This was a habit Doctor Hurbalife employed whenever he was excited, and it now served to warm him up to the subject at hand. Thus stimulated, he continued with his dissertation.

"Elementary my dear Beach. Patient comes to doctor. Patient has complaint. Doctor offers cure. Patient takes cure. All is well.

"Now let us make of this happy couple, a *ménage à trois*. Enter science, poking her snoopy nose under the covers. Not so fast, she says. Is this a true cure? Or is it merely an illusion? Let us examine. Check—she dissects the variables. Check—she analyzes the results. Check—she computes the probabilities. Whir. Click. Snap. She declares—according to her calculations, which have an ought point three percent chance of error—that this case may still end up in total disaster. That likelihood, she pronounces with grim satisfaction, is precisely fifty-three point two seven five. Bingo! Doctor loses confidence in cure. Patient loses confidence in doctor. Patient loses cure. And there you have it." He waved his arms majestically as he concluded his argument. *"Quod. Ergo. Propter. Et hoc!"*

"You're right on the money there, H."

"Of course I am. It is indisputable. It is irrefutable. It is unsurmountable. It is, in short, the only possible outcome. And whom, you may ask—Yes, whom do you ask—whom do we have to blame for this devilish turn of the screw? Ourselves! None other. It is all our own fault! For in our haste to hop on the scientific bandwagon, we have abandoned the principles of him who made us what we ought to be today."

"Hippocrates?"

"God."

"Of course. But I guess we're stuck with it now. I mean, the cat is out of the bag, and there doesn't seem to be any way of getting her back in."

"Nonsense!" exclaimed Hurbalife vehemently pounding his fist on my table. "Rubbish, poppycock and flibberty-jib! Of course we can. Do you really believe that we—we who are empowered by the Almighty Himself—are bereft of any weapons with which to fight this heretical monster? No! No! No, I tell you my friend! We still have a few tricks up our sleeves."

"Tricks?"

I could hardly believe myself! Here was this lunatic, completely off his rocker, and I—I was listening to him! Listening, not with the interest one might attach to an unusual case of dementia praecox, but with the actual hope—expectation even—that there was something he could tell me. Something that was going to help me out of my troubles. Could he? Or was it just that, weakened by my recent failures, I had fallen victim to his folly? I honestly could not tell. But this much I did know. Whatever he had up his sleeve, I had to see it.

"Nothing easier," he said smiling broadly. "It is simply a matter of setting one's plow to till the virgin fields.

"Virgin fields."

"Those fields where science has yet to cast her evil seed."

"Where are those fields, you ask? Everywhere, I answer! We are surrounded by them. But in our eagerness to look up to the mountains afar, we have missed the treasures beneath our feet. *Captis trifolia*—the lowly roadside weed. *Hirado suculans*—humble pond dweller. Hawthorn, vervain, ginseng, golden heliotrope. All great remedies once. Tried and true, but now forgotten in the pell mell rush to scrabble before the feet of a new idol. Raise them up again, my boy. Bring them back into the fold. Believe me, you will not regret it. They did not fail Hippocrates. They did not fail Vesalius. They will not fail you

"You mean—?"

"Precisely!" He raised his index finger above his head, brandishing it like a sword. "They will succeed for that very reason. Because they have been forgotten! Because they have never been reported in a medical journal. Because they have never been randomly tested in a double blind. *Because they have never been discussed on public radio!*" And bringing his finger crashing down to skewer his imaginary opponent, he brought his argument to its victorious conclusion.

Daft or not, I had to admit it. The old boy had a point. Maybe putting the magic back in my medicine might not be as difficult as I had feared. It was simply a matter of playing the right cards. The merits of Hurbalife's plan were obvious. Its defects appeared nonexistent.

Then and there I made myself a vow. I would put his principle to use as quickly as possible. This, I had reason to hope, might be quite soon, for something had recently come into my possession that could prove to be he perfect instrument for carrying out my new intentions.

Last week Bill Patch had presented me with a collection of his grandfather's medical effects. He had found them when cleaning his attic. Doctor Patch had been Dumster's only doctor from about eighteen ninety until the early twenties. Bill had no use for them, and he gave them to me thinking I might find them a curiosity.

There were several books, an assortment of glass containers, and some instruments. The books—full of discussions on arcane diseases that had passed from the scene long before I arrived, made for interesting reading, but I had little use for rest of the stuff. Now, however, seen in the light of Doctor Hurbalife's lesson, one of them in particular piqued my interest. I hastened home to retrieve it from the trash barrel, to which it had been thoughtlessly consigned.

It was a smallish black box, rectangular in shape and slightly larger than a cigar case. Inside, resting on a bed of purple velvet, was a black-handled object about the size of a flashlight. To one end of the object was attached an electric cord. At the other was a hole. Nestled alongside this object was an assortment of hollow glass rods, each one of which had a metallic end that could be inserted into the hole in the handle. Accompanying the collection was a booklet which explained that what I possessed was the original Super Marvel Violet Ray, which, when used according to the instruction, was guaranteed to cure everything from brain fag to dropsy.

I removed one of the rods from its resting place—it was shaped like a rake—stuck it into the handle, and plugged in the cord. The Super Marvel buzzed for several seconds and then emitted a lovely violet light which flashed back and forth along the length of the tube. I applied the rake lightly to my hand. There was a crackle of electricity as the light spread to my palm. This was accompanied by a pleasant tingling sensation. I passed the rake several times across my scalp. This, as the instructions stated, was its intended use. I could almost feel the hairs already beginning to sprout. It was an exhilarating feeling. Convinced of the untapped restorative powers lying within this remarkable little machine, I could hardly wait to try it out.

Chapter 16

Sunrise

"Beach?"

"Yes."

"This is Sunrise. I hate to bother you, but I have a problem."

"What is it?"

"My stomach."

"What about your stomach?"

"It hurts."

"How bad?"

"Not too bad."

"Are you vomiting?"

"No."

"Do you have any diarrhea?"

"A little."

"How's your appetite?"

"Fine."

"What have you eaten?"

"Yogurt."

"What else?"

"Nothing else."

"Just yogurt?"

"Yes."

"That's your culprit. Cut it out for a few days, and I'm sure everything will be fine."

"I can't"

"Why not?"

"Yogurt is all I can eat."

"You mean anything except yogurt makes you sick?"

"Well—in a way—yes."

"What do you mean *in a way?*"

"If I eat anything else, I get depressed."

"I'm afraid I don't understand."

"It's my allergies."

"Sunrise, have you been to Berkeley?"

"That's what I wanted to talk to you about."

"I think that's an excellent idea. Why don't you come in this afternoon."

"I can't."

"Is something wrong with your car?"

"No—I can't leave the house."

"Why not?"

"Because of my allergies."

"This is not making a lot of sense, Sunrise."

"If you would just come see me, I could explain it a lot better. It's a long story."

"I'll be right over."

"Thanks, Beach. I knew I could count on you."

Sunrise Holbode had moved to Dumster about the same time as I. Also like me she had emigrated from Berkeley in search of life the pure and simple. She had, however, been rather more faithful to the principle than I. Her home was a small log cabin in the outer reaches of Stedsville. There she raised her own food, cut her own fuel, made her own clothes, and earned what cash she needed by selling yarn she spun out her sheep's wool. With these thrifty measures, and the help of a trust fund from her father, who was the president of Wells Fargo Bank, Sunrise was able to live successfully off the land.

Sunrise did not admit the medical profession much into her life. She preferred natural remedies for her afflictions, which, since she was young and lived a healthy life, were as susceptible to such ministrations as anything I had to offer. Occasionally, however, she had trouble with asthma, and on such occasions she would come to me. My tenure in Berkeley gave me a passport to her trust.

Even though it was mid-April, there was still a foot of snow on the ground in Stedsville, and Sunrise's steep driveway, improbable under the best of circumstances, was now quite impossible. I got out of my car at the bottom of the hill and trudged the half mile to her cabin. As I came around the last corner, and the cabin came in view, I realized that Sunrise had not been exaggerating about a long story.

Sticking out of a window was one, and protruding from the top of the chimney was the second, of a pair of large metallic tubes. Attached to the end of the lower tube was a boxlike receptacle from which came a low humming noise. Out of the upper one came a thin stream of wispy smoke. Snow was piled in front of the cabin. There was a makeshift tunnel that led to the house. I entered the tunnel and knocked on the door.

"Come in," said a voice from the other side. I opened the door and stepped in. I was in a small entry. There was another door in front of me. On the wall hung several scrub uniforms. On the floor were some paper slippers.

"I'm sorry about this, Beach," said the voice, "but would you take off your clothes and put on one of those suits?"

I did as she requested and knocked again. Sunrise, dressed in an identical outfit, opened the door and bade me enter. Except for a large furnacelike structure in one corner, the cabin was completely devoid of furniture. Connected to the structure, which was emitting the humming sound I had heard outside, were the two ducts. On one of its sides was a large rectangular pan in which sat some kind of filter. At the bottom was a glass bottle. Sunrise had evidently been tending to this contraption before my arrival, for she returned to the filter and began tinkering with it. After a minute or so of this activity, she nodded in satisfaction and waved me to a seat on the floor.

"You know how much trouble I've been having with my asthma recently," she began. "Well, when I was out in Berkeley, I ran into someone from my old collective. I told her about my trouble, and she said that she had been in a similar situation with her headaches. She had been to three chiropractors, an acupuncturist, and four therapists, and none of them had done her any good. But then she went to a clinical ecologist, and he fixed her up."

Sunrise had presented me over the years with many unorthodox treatments, and part of our agreement was that I never questioned her on them, but as clinical ecology was a concept with which I was unfamiliar, I indicated that an explanation might be in order for her stick-in-the-mud physician.

"A clinical ecologist specializes in treating allergies," she said.

"I see," I said, not seeing at all. Sunrise, noting my perplexity, continued.

"Not ordinary allergies. Environmental allergies—like air and water and stuff like that."

"Oh yes, stuff like that. And what did this clinical ecologist do for you?"

"First he did a bunch of tests. I mean, no disrespect, Beach, but he's got it all over you when it comes to ordering. He tested my blood for vitamins and minerals. He tested my skin for sensitivities. He tested my T cells and my B cells and all kinds of other cells I don't even know what they were. He put a patch on my tongue to determine my absorption of toxins. He even took clippings of my hair and analyzed them. He was very thorough.

"Very."

"Yup. It cost me five thousand dollars, and because your elitist AMA doesn't recognize clinical ecology as a legitimate specialty, my insurance wouldn't pay. But it was worth every penny! I got this detoxification machine as part of the package." She pointed to the contraption. "I call him Lazarus. He's a little noisy at night, but I just love him." She patted Lazarus affectionately on the side.

Lazarus hummed.

"You certainly look made for each other. But tell me, what does Lazarus do?"

"Well, as Doctor Kolrabi explained it, there are people—like me for one—who have bodies that have not yet evolved from earlier times, when there was no pollution in the air, no poisons in the water, and no chemicals in the food. So we develop allergies to them."

"Like your asthma?"

"Like my asthma. And much more. These allergies can cause all kinds of problems. Doctor Kolrabi said there isn't any symptom that couldn't be caused by environmental allergy. Fatigue, dizziness, headaches, arthritis—even depression."

"I didn't know you were depressed."

"Neither did I until Doctor Kolrabi went over all the things that were wrong with me."

"And the treatment—"

"Is to remove the allergens from your environment. The way Doctor Kolrabi put it, I'm allergic to the twentieth century."

"And this device takes you back to the purer days of yesteryear."

"In a way. Look—" She donned a pair of gloves, went over to Lazarus, and unscrewed the glass jar. It contained a small amount of white powder. "See that stuff. That's just since you came in. It's your contaminants." Then she went over to the other side of the machine, opened a valve, and drew out some water. "And here—

this is my distilled water. I do everything with distilled water now—I even make my yogurt with it."

"Ah yes, the yogurt."

"It's to keep yeast out of my system. Dr. Kolrabi found out my worst allergy was yeast."

"I didn't realize that yeast was a twentieth century germ."

"It isn't. That's the amazing thing. You remember those yeast infections I had last year after you gave me the antibiotics for my bronchitis? That's what triggered all this. You see the yeast infection—I'm not blaming you Beach. There was no way you could have known—was sort of the catalyst that depressed my immune system so that my resistance went down, and that's when the allergies set in."

"All from a little penicillin."

"I thought you'd be impressed. I feel better now than I have in ages. Perfect, actually. Except for one thing."

"What's that?"

"Doctor Kolrabi said that after six months of treatment I might be able to go outside for ten minutes at a time, and that he expected me to be cured in about two years. It's—"

"A small price to pay for one's health."

"I know. Still—" she paused, and her voice trailed off. There was a wistful look in her eyes. Apparently life in her cocoon had been less than totally enchanting. I saw my opening.

"Sunrise," I said, "believe it or not, I think I can help you out of your predicament."

"You? What do you know about clinical ecology?"

"All that I need to. Just give me a chance. After I've given you the treatment I have in mind, I am confidant that you will be as free as a bird."

"But what—"

"It's in the car. I'll be right back. Don't go away."

"Hardly."

I went back and fetched the Super Marvel.

"What's that?" she asked, eyeing it suspiciously.

"This, Sunrise, is the Super Marvel Violet Ray. It was used by doctors at the turn of the century to treat all kinds of diseases. Conditions like neurasthenia and febricula and—"

"Allergies?"

"Yes—allergies too. In fact, it could treat just about anything. But it was abandoned by the medical profession. It worked *too* well.

It threatened to put us out of business. Kind of like an automobile that never broke down. I happened onto it by chance not too long ago, and I've been most impressed with its abilities. It relies on the faradic principle of galvanic stimulation, rechanneling the energy of your biorhythms. It's completely natural. But the best thing about it is—the Super Marvel Violet Ray is not approved by the AMA. In fact, if any of my colleagues found out I was using it, they'd run me out of town. My first allegiance, however, is to my patients, so I'll use it, no matter what the others say. And I'll guarantee you, the Super Marvel Violet Ray works. Just a couple of treatments, and your yeast troubles will be history."

I took the Super Marvel out of its box and plugged it in. "Here, give me your hand."

Sunrise hesitated.

"Don't be afraid. It won't bite."

Cautiously she extended her hand. I gave her a few passes at low power.

"It tingles," she giggled, "and it makes me feel a little silly."

"Good. Now, take off your clothes."

"All of them?"

"C'mon Sunrise," I said, "Do you want to fool around, or do you want to take the cure?"

Sunrise undressed. I turned the Super Marvel up to full power. Sparks flew out from the base. I placed the probe on top of her head and began working it in a circular fashion down around her ears to her neck.

"Ouch!" she cried. "That hurts. Are you sure it isn't too strong?"

"No pain, Sunrise, no gain. You have a serious condition here. It's going to require all that this little baby can give to get you rid of it."

"But—are you sure this is going to work?"

"Positive. In fact, I think we may be getting some results very soon." I continued to work the Super Marvel down her body. When I got to her umbilicus, Sunrise made a move to push my hand away.

"I'm not so sure about this, Beach. This whole thing is getting a little weird."

"Excellent," I said. Things were progressing nicely.

Ignoring her attempt to resist, I continued to ray until I had covered every single part of Sunrise Holbode's body. When I put the Super Marvel down, it was glowing, but no more so than Sunrise, who had turned beet red from head to toe.

"Now." I said. "How do you feel?"

"Like a fool."

"Like an idiot?"

"Yes."

"A *complete* idiot?"

"Almost."

"Then we're *almost* done." I took up the Super Marvel and placed it again on her scalp. "One more pass will do it, I think."

She pushed it away." No," she said. "That won't be necessary."

"Are you sure? I wouldn't want the allergy to come back again."

"It won't."

I put the Super Marvel back in its box, put on my clothes, and said goodbye to Sunrise. It was a most satisfactory experience, I thought as I drove back to the hospital. Most satisfactory indeed. No doubt about it. This little gadget was going to fix a lot of patients—and one doctor's practice in the bargain.

Chapter 17

Love

The people of Dumster are pretty good when it comes to loyalty, and any suggestion made by their doctor, outlandish as it might seem, is given all possible respect. But they are considerably less endowed in their stocks of imagination and flexibility. They tend to be rather fixed in their ways.

When, for example, Lucien Comstock, after some thirty years of spending his winter in the traditional *rouge et noir*, suddenly appeared one day sporting a brand new coat of which the red checks had been replaced by green, tongues were set to wagging that his appetite for the new server at Nap's Lunch was more than gastronomical. And when old man Contremond replaced the Red Man display rack that had occupied prime real estate on his checkout counter with Kodiak, there was much talk about what was this town coming to.

So they accepted the Super Marvel's violet rays without protest. But they were unable to take fully to the idea that a machine which emitted purple sparks would be of greater benefit to them than a pill, and thus they failed to give it the unquestioning devotion necessary for full effectiveness. Consequently, although the Super Marvel proved to be a useful addition to my therapeutic armamentarium, I was never able to duplicate the dramatic success I had achieved with Sunrise Holbode.

I except from this the Peabodians, who almost to a man, were wholly enamored of the machine's healing powers. Whether it was because they were by nature more enlightened than their fellow townspeople, or whether alcohol had rendered them less prone to critical evaluation, I cannot say, but it was undeniable that no sooner had I tried it upon one, than the rest flocked immediately to my office to take the Super Marvel cure.

It appeared for a time that I might be able to support my practice almost exclusively on this small but active band, a possibility that, just a few months earlier, would have curdled my blood. But wiser and more tolerant now, I was able to accept their patronage with equanimity. Unfortunately, not long after my visit with Sunrise, an event occurred which brought the reign of the Super Marvel Violet Ray to an abrupt and irrevocable end.

To say that Eddie Kapinsky was one of Gola's regulars does not do justice to his loyalty. Eddie Kapinsky *was* Gola's. He was its Rock of Gibraltar. Eddie Kapinsky was the bulwark upon which this venerable institution relied, carrying it forward when it prospered in good times and propping it up when it foundered in bad. With Eddie Kapinsky, Gola's was a formidable drinking establishment. Without him, it was just another bar.

A hard working, hard drinking Pole, Eddie spent the day from sunrise to sundown at whatever manual labor he could find, and the night, from sundown to closing, at Gola's. Then, when the last customer had left, when the bar counter had been wiped clean, and when all the bottles put back on the shelf, Eddie Kapinsky headed toward home. Sweet it may be, but the venerable destination was one, more often than not, that Eddie failed to reach. This was owing less to any disruptive influence his imbibitions had on Eddie's navigating abilities, which, diminished as they may have been, would have been sufficient to get him to his house, situated only two doors down from Gola's. It was, rather, more due to a lack of commitment on Eddie's part in attaining the purported goal, where, regardless of the hour, awaiting him at the family fireside, was his beloved Sophie.

Sophie Kapinsky was a small woman. Her deficiency in stature, however, was more than compensated for by her fiery temper and an unshakable determination to see through whatever she set out to do. When Sophie took to a cause, she was a formidable warrior. And when she was in battle she was always equipped with her two favorite weapons, a razor sharp tongue and a pair of long knitting needles, both of which she could wield with a ferocity which made her much respected.

One of the causes Sophie took up on a regular basis was the improvement of her husband's character, which, she had long since determined, was deficient in every possible respect. In Sophie's eyes, her Eddie was a child, and a miscreant one at that. And as such he was in need of constant discipline, which she provided on all possible occasions, relying heavily, to reinforce her improvement efforts, on the assistance of the aforementioned educational devices. Those who were acquainted with Eddie said he drank too much. Those who knew Sophie said he didn't drink enough.

Eddie Kapinsky was a quiet, introspective man. He was not much given to vanity, and he did not particularly care about his appearance. With one exception. When Nature had created Eddie, she had assembled him generally along rather plain lines, short like his Sophie, and with nondescript features. But she had, perhaps in an exact calculation of the effect, stuck upon this most ordinary package a most extraordinary wrapping. Up above his thin wispy eyebrows, and up above his flat narrow forehead rose a magnificent shock of bright red curly hair. Shining atop Eddie's humble pate like a beacon set upon some unadorned rock, it was truly something to behold.

Eddie knew his hair was a thing of special grandeur. He had a sense that, although he possessed it, he did not really own it. It was like some public treasure for which he, Eddie, was the caretaker.

Eddie took his responsibility seriously. Whatever of his hard-earned money he didn't spend on liquor, he used on his hair. He bought special vitamins guaranteed to promote its health and expensive potions promising to enhance its lustre. And every morning he groomed it meticulously with a secret tonic of his own concoction until each strand positively shone. Crooning and cooing like a mother hen to her brood, he carefully coaxed the whole lot into a veritable mountain of hair that towered almost half a foot above his forehead, producing a majestic coiffure that gave Eddie an impression of substance much greater than that usually attributed to one who stood five-foot-five in his stocking feet.

One day, following a night when Gola's had been forced to close early due to a fire in the basement, Eddie awakened unusually sober and noticed a rash behind his right ear. The cause of this dermatological disruption, as best I could determine, was a tendency of the part in question to remain, for hours on end, in close approximation to the sidewalk outside his favorite establishment. Despite a liberal application of Bag Balm and vigorous bouts of scratching, Eddie was unable to cure the pesky thing. As the rash appeared to be encroaching dangerously upon his precious baby, Eddie was most eager to rid himself of the affliction.

It seemed to me quite probable that with the simple expedient of giving this side a rest for a few days in favor of the other, the problem would clear up quite nicely on its own. I considered it, therefore, an ideal candidate for the Super Marvel's rays.

I am not quite sure what went wrong. It may have been that the aged circuitry of the Super Marvel was unable to keep up with current demand, or it may have been that Eddie's pomade affected the ray's conductive properties. At any rate, after a few uneventful passes, there came a loud cracking noise from the handle, and before I knew what had happened, Eddie's Kapinsky's pride and joy was a mass of flames.

Eddie recovered without permanent injury, although for six months he was only seen in public with a wool cap pulled tightly over his eyes. The Super Marvel did not fare as well. Word of Eddie's experience spread through town with all the rapidity of the fire that had scalped him, and so it was that, even had I been able to resurrect it, I knew I would never again be able to use my miracle working machine. The Super Marvel Violet Ray was dead.

Doctors come in all kinds of varieties. There are ologists and oscopists. There are icians and itioners. There are old ones, and there are young ones. Some are ambitious, others lazy. A fair number are greedy. Equal in number are charitable. But all these specimens are merely variations on one of the two basic themes that define the medical practitioner.

The first, and by far the more common specimen is the loyalist. In medical school they are the ones who attend every lecture and hang on each word of professorial wisdom. As practitioners, they are content to ply their trade tucked safely into the mainstream of medicine. Whatever is the vogue is their dictum. Anything not strictly according to Hoyle is anathema. They are a uniform product of well-tested reliability. They are solid, trustworthy doctors.

Then there are the others. Theirs is a different drummer. As students they can be readily identified by their tendency to miss morning classes and to nap during those that are held immediately after lunch. Attracted to the side streams of medicine, they are the ones who dare to be different. Often they are brilliant. Occasionally foolhardy. Sometimes they are unreliable. Always they are unpredictable.

I am not a loyalist.

Although saddened by the loss of the Super Marvel Violet Ray, the experience did not discourage me. If anything it emboldened me to trod again the untrod ways, testing, and perhaps defining along the way, the new frontiers of medicine.

It happened that Sunrise, as thanks for my having rid her of her allergies, had given me something that provided just such an opportunity. It was a book called *Loving Your Ills to Death*, written by Doctor Ingrid Celeste, a holistic healer who lives on Mount Shasta. Doctor Celeste leads a small but devoted band of disciples known as Shastiferians. Shastiferians believe their chosen mountain has special powers. That from its slopes emits an energy force with great healing and restorative ability. Most Shastiferians live at the base of Shasta, although a few heretics have migrated south to Mendocino and the Santa Cruz Mountains, which, they claim, have similar abilities.

In her book the author espouses the belief that diseases are caused, not by germs or poisons or the general wear and tear of life, but by a deficiency of love. This is no ordinary love, of the variety we give to mates, relatives, or our favorite deity. It is a more important love—that which we give ourselves. According to Doctor Celeste, when a person doesn't love his self enough, self goes into a kind of immunological snit. It mopes around dark alleys feeling blue and being generally susceptible to plagues and pestilences. We are all subject to the love deficit she proclaims. Even the most confirmed narcissist will, at one time or another, fall prey to self-neglect.

As Doctor Celeste says, "You can love some of yourself all of the time, and you can love all of yourself some of the time, but you can't love all of yourself all of the time."

The antidote for love deficiency is love augmentation. *Loving Your Ills to Death* gave numerous examples of how love augmentation works, proving its powers in curing everything from hypoglycemia to chronic fatigue syndrome.

Awakening all my dormant California sensibilities, I found myself relating to love augmentation from the start. Here was a treatment that relied, not on the oppressive ministrations of elitist authority, but on the assertion of one's own inner spiritual strength. Hardly had I finished the book when I made a vow that henceforth every patient who came through my door would be love-augmented to the limit of our mutual abilities.

My inaugural patient was Hiram Stedrock. Hiram had a bump on his nose.

Hiram Stedrock is the sole surviving member of the Stedrock clan. He lives on the family farm in Stedsville, a much-depleted community founded by his great-great-great-grandfather Ephrain Stedrock, who cleared the land in 1755. Like all the Stedrocks before him, Hiram is a farmer. Also like his ancestors, Hiram has a pretty matter-of-fact view of things. Things, to Hiram, are in one of two states. Either they are fixed or they are broke. If it's fixed, Hiram lets it be. If it's broke, Hiram tries to fix it. If he can't fix it, he'll do the best he can with it. And when he can't do with it, Hiram does the best he can without it.

Philosophically speaking, Hiram's beliefs would be considered a branch, not so much of another tree, as in an altogether different forest from that on which grew the views of Doctor Celeste. To offer my new delicacy to Sunrise Holbode would have been like feeding pablum to a baby. Serving it to Hiram was like trying *champignon-au-vin* on Rover.

It was, in short, a challenging case. But challenge is what this business was all about, and I felt up to it. Dispensing with preliminaries, I sprang from the board and plunged right in.

"Hiram," I said, "you don't love yourself enough."

Hiram looked at me with an intent expression that confirmed his reception of the message I had just transmitted. But other than a slight furrow of his brow, he did not immediately offer anything in reply.

Hiram was a methodical man, and whether he was plowing a field or processing advice, he proceeded along every course in the same meticulous manner. Hiram also believed that words were a precious commodity, and as such should not be wasted in mere conversation. Accustomed to both of Hiram's estimable features, I waited for his response. After several minutes my patience was rewarded.

"Huh?"

It was a large bite I had fed him, and Hiram's palate was not accustomed to fare of the sort I had just provided.

"That's what your trouble is," I explained. "Self-love. You don't have enough of it."

Hiram repeated his response.

His digestion had not improved with this last morsel. It appeared that Hiram would have to be spoon fed.

"How you feel about yourself in general, and how you feel about each part of you in particular, has a substantial effect on your health. Your body is composed of billions of individual cells. Every one of them is a complete living organism. Every one has wants and needs of its own. While the feelings of one small cell are not as manifest as those of the whole body, they are no less important, for they constitute, in the aggregate, the state of the Stedrock. Should any one of these anonymous little souls feel that it has been slighted—perhaps by an action so insignificant that you did not even give it second thought, it will become—let us say—down."

"Down?"

"Down. Down as the bottom of a well. Down as a sun that's set. Down as a dog who's lost his coon."

"Down."

"Yes. Down. And a down cell doesn't work as well as one that's on its feed. A down cell is, well—susceptible."

"Doc?" he asked quietly. "You been talking to Hurbalife?"

"Susceptible to something not going right," I continued, choosing to consider this last question rhetorical. "If, for example, a liver cell is out of sorts at some chunk of lard you have thoughtlessly foisted upon it, it might retaliate with a dose of colic. Or if the tip of your big toe feels its style is being cramped by a tight boot, gout could be the result.

"Now, let us take your problem. This bump. If it turns out to be only a pimple, I would say you have but a minor deficit. If however, as looks to be the case, it is skin cancer, your love balance sheet must be substantially in the red. Hiram, just how *have* you been relating to your nose recently?"

Hiram, whose linguistic repertoire was as limited as his proclivity to use it, could muster no more than a hapless shrug by way of answer. It was clear I was going to have to help him work this out.

"Consider, for example, any indiscretions you may have inflicted on the old sniffer. An occasional after-dinner cigar. A bit of limburger. Or perhaps you have used it in the detection of socks needing to be washed? Any one of these could certainly upset the olfactory applecart."

"Hmmm," conceded Hiram.

Thus encouraged, I forged ahead. "Perhaps the problem is more of a physical nature. Do your glasses pinch a little? Have you left it out in the sun too long? Have you, perchance, been picking?"

"No-ope," he said after some consideration.

My current line of questioning was not yielding much in the way of results. It was time to attack from a different angle. "Hiram," I asked fixing him straight in the eyes with my most penetrating look, "how do you feel about your nose?"

Hiram stared at me dumbly. The blow had struck too close to the mark. I struck again.

"When you look in the mirror, are you pleased by what you see? Or do you wish it was a different nose? A little slimmer? A tad longer? Or maybe sporting a curve along the aquiline line?"

"Never thought about it."

"Never?"

"Nope."

"Then I suppose," I said, honing in on the heart of the matter, "that you never give it an affectionate little rub now and then, or tell it, just out of the blue, Nose, you handsome devil you, I don't know what I'd do without you. In my book you're one all right proboscis."

"Don't recollect it."

My suspicions were confirmed. "Hiram," I said triumphantly, "that's your problem."

What could he say? He didn't even try.

"You see, Hiram, the nose is a tender organ. The nose is a delicate organ. The nose is a—*sensitive* organ. It needs to be appreciated. It needs to be wanted. It needs to be loved. And what have you been doing? Taking it for granted. Treating your nose as if it were nothing more than a bump on a log. This cancer is your nose's way of saying, 'Look at me. Pay attention to me. Care about me!' I suggest that after we get the cancer off, you and your nose spend some time together, just the two of you. Smell the roses. Go for long walks in the woods. Take in the fresh air. Treat it to a little *salon de bain*. It will make all the difference in the world. I promise you."

"You sure, Doc?" Hiram was having difficulty, as well he might. It was hard, after so many years of nasal neglect, to own up to his abusive behavior.

"I'm afraid there is really no other explanation Hiram. The evidence is incontrovertible. It's as plain as the nose on your face."

"'Cept—" He looked at me uncertainly.

"Except for what, Hiram?"

"Mind you," he said slowly, "I don't understand much of what you've said. It's way above me. But if you're right about this business, I'd 'a thought—" Embarrassed at this outburst of verbiage, Hiram flushed suddenly and became silent.

"You'd have thought what, Hiram? Go on, out with it. Don't be afraid. It's only words."

Hiram winced. Then he blurted out. "I'd 'a thought you'd have the same problem yourself."

"I—I beg your pardon?"

"Not meaning disrespect, Doc, but when it comes to not treating a nose right, well—I'd guess yours has been in a pretty sorry place."

It was my turn not to understand. "What are you talking about, Hiram. Where has my nose been that it doesn't belong?"

"Stuck in someone else's business."

Chapter 18

The Mammogram

Samantha Sticklethwaite is a particular person. I do not mean this in the sense that one refers to an ordinary person such as you or I or the postal carrier—who is particular because he is not anybody else. Samantha Sticklethwaite is not an ordinary particular person.

When Samantha Sticklethwaite brushes her teeth in the morning, she positions herself exactly two feet from the mirror. She opens her mouth exactly one and a half inches. She places the brush at the base of the right lower wisdom tooth. Starting on the upbeat, she brushes the tooth in twelve graceful strokes. At precisely the stroke of twelve she goes on to the next tooth, and she repeats the same procedure. It takes Samantha Sticklethwaite exactly five minutes to brush her teeth, which is exactly what the dentist told her it should take if she did a proper job. Which she does. Samantha Sticklethwaite *always* does a proper job.

When Samantha Sticklethwaite does her hair in the morning, she stands exactly two feet in front of the mirror. She parts her hair exactly in the center. She places the brush on the right hand side of the part. Starting on the downstroke, she brushes the length of her hair in twelve graceful strokes. She repeats the procedure on the left side. Then she ties it up with a clasp. The clasp matches her shirt, her pants, her socks, and her underwear. This is exactly what Samantha Sticklethwaite's mother told her she should do to look just right. Which she does. Samantha Sticklethwaite *always* looks just right.

When Samantha Sticklethwaite arrives at her desk in the morning, she divides her books into two sets. Each set is lined up exactly with the other and equidistant from the middle. On the left side, in alphabetical order are *Brothers Karamazov. Great Expectations. Middlemarch. Pride and Prejudice.* It is the required reading. On the right side, similarly ordered—*Lady Chatterly's Lover. Madame Bovary. On the Road. 1984.* These books—the right side ones—if the youth of Dumster had any idea what lay inside them, which they don't because they are the *elective* reading, they might form a very different opinion about their English teacher. But that is not the point now. The point now is what kind of particular person she is. Which is this. Samantha Sticklethwaite is a *very particular* particular person.

"There are two ways of doing things—" Samantha Sticklethwaite is fond of saying. (I say fond in the sense that she uses the expression frequently, but as Ms. Sticklethwaite, would point out if she were to read this, fondness is a word properly reserved for objects which have some capacity for reciprocating. It does not belong in a sentence describing a person's linguistic propensities. Although I would ordinarily defer to Ms. Sticklethwaite on all matters semantic, I have used the word advisedly and in full knowledge of its consequences.) "the right way, and every other way." Samantha Sticklethwaite believes in doing things *the right way*.

One of things considered the right way by Samantha Sticklethwaite is checkups. Whether it is her car or her furnace or her body, Samantha Sticklethwaite is convinced that routine inspection of the parts is a good idea. Which it is.

When things are going slow in the office, when time is too much on the hands and not enough on the bills, when disease has gone on a holiday, and all the troubles have been packed up in an old kit bag and flown away, doctors have one surefire way to jump start their idle practice buggy.

Not enough sickness knocking at the door? Invite in the well. Too few symptoms hanging around? Take up with the asymptomatic. Health maintenance, the greatest boon to the practice of medicine since invention of the placebo, is the trusted standby we use to get the juices flowing and the turnstiles clicking.

The value of health maintenance to a clean-living patient like Samantha Sticklethwaite is a matter of considerable debate within the profession. What is beyond dispute, however, is its value to those who provide it.

In health maintenance there is no inconvenience of the unexplainable symptom. In health maintenance there is no worry over the elusive diagnosis. Health maintenance is played with the doctors's rules on the doctor's home court. And because it doesn't end until it succeeds, everybody comes out of health maintenance with something.

When Samantha Sticklethwaite came in for her checkup, she brought with her a list. At the top of the list was,
1. mammogram

"It is my understanding, Doctor Conger, that I am approaching—excuse me—I will soon reach an age when breast cancer is a common problem. When it will be, in fact, the cancer I am most likely to contract. Furthermore I believe that it is the disease most likely to cause my premature demise."

"That is correct."

"It is also my understanding that the chances of being cured of breast cancer are substantially increased if it can be detected by a mammogram before it is large enough to feel."

"Quite true."

"And that newer mammographic techniques have considerably reduced the risk of one's acquiring breast cancer from the radiation used for the test."

"True again."

"But they have not eliminated it altogether."

"Not quite."

"So that there is little doubt mammograms will be of benefit to me—"

"Little indeed."

"—at some point in my life. My question is," she lowered her glasses and looked down at her list before returning her steady gaze to me, "exactly when does the benefit accrued by the early detection of a breast cancer outweigh the risk that repeated mammograms might induce one."

"That is the question."

"Thank you, Doctor Conger. What is the answer?"

"The answer. As the man says, you pays your money, and you takes your choice. If you know what I mean."

"I believe I do. As always, Doctor Conger, you are entertaining. But the purpose of my visit is not one of pleasure. I would like to know if this is the year I should have my first mammogram."

"Excuse me. When to have the first mammogram. Well—at the age of fifty—"

"I am forty, Doctor Conger."

"Forty."

"Today is my fortieth birthday."

"Of course. Happy Birthday Ms. Sticklethwaite."

"Thank you, Doctor Conger."

"And you want to know if you should have a mammogram."

"Today."

"Today."

"Precisely."

"On your fortieth birthday."

"Yes."

"That is a very good question."

"I pride myself on the quality of my questions."

"There is some controversy on this subject, Ms Sticklethwaite."

"I am aware of the controversy, Doctor Conger."

"You are."

"I am."

"Of course."

"If I choose not to get a mammogram, I run a risk of not finding in time a breast cancer that could be cured."

"You do."

"What chance is that?"

"It's a small chance."

"How small, Doctor Conger?"

"About one in a thousand."

"And if I decide to have a mammogram, the cancer you find might still be incurable, and all I will have accomplished is spending more time and money with my doctors. Nothing personal, Doctor Conger, but that is not what I intend to do. In addition there is the risk that the mammogram might eventually cause the very cancer it is intended to cure."

"A very small risk."

"Less than one in a thousand?"

"Probably."

"Probably?"

"Less than one in a thousand."

"So it depends on which cancer I worry about more, the one I might get, or the one you might give me. Am I correct?"

"You could say that."

"I did."

"Yes, you did."

"The risk, Doctor Conger."

"The risk. Well, the older you get, the more the scales favor the one you get over the one a mammogram gives you."

"At forty, Doctor Conger."

"It's a close call."

"I appreciate that, Doctor Conger, but it's a call I have to make."

"In your case, Ms. Sticklethwaite, I would say yes."

Samantha Sticklethwaite got her mammogram. After I got the report, I called her up.

"I'd like you to come in for a breast examination," I told her.

"I don't understand. I thought the mammogram was better than an examination."

"It usually is."

"Usually?"

"Your mammogram showed something in the right breast."

"What did it show?"

"A slight irregularity. It's nothing really."

"I thought you said it was something."

"It is something, but it's nothing."

"It's a something that's a nothing?"

"You could say that."

"Yes, Doctor Conger. Can you explain, please, why you want to examine this something that's nothing?"

"I'd like to see if I can feel anything?"

"You want to examine my something that's nothing to see if you can feel anything?"

"Would you do me a favor Ms. Sticklethwaite?"

"Of course, Doctor Conger."

"Make an appointment."

Samantha Sticklethwaite came in for her appointment. I examined her breast.

"I can't feel anything," I told her.

"Then there isn't anything to the something of mine that's really nothing?"

"Probably not."

"*Probably* not?"

"Well—there might be."

"I thought you said—"

"I reviewed the mammograms with our radiologists. One of them didn't think it was much of anything."

"One of them?"

"Right. Another one wasn't sure. The third one was suspicious."

"You have an untrustworthy radiologist?"

"No. What I mean is that she was suspicious that there might be something. She said she saw a mammogram once very much like yours, and that's what it turned out to be."

"What did it turn out to be?"

"Something."

"What kind of something?"

"A tumor."

"So this might be breast cancer."

"That's very unlikely."

"What is likely then?"

"That it's not much of anything."

"Excuse me, Doctor Conger, but didn't we just go through this?"

"I'm sorry. Most likely it's fibrocystic disease."

"Most likely?"

"Quite probably. But we can never guarantee anything you know."

"Of that I am quite aware, thank you. What do we do next?"

"We could do nothing."

"Nothing about a cancer?"

"Well, we'd watch it pretty closely, of course."

"I don't think so."

"You don't think I should watch it?"

"I like you, Doctor Conger, but I don't want you staring at my breast all day long."

"Of course. What I mean is that we'd recheck the mammogram to see if it changed."

"When would you do that?"

"In about six months.

"So we watch this something that probably isn't anything for six months to see if it becomes breast cancer?"

"Or three if you prefer."

"That doesn't sound much different."

"It's a difference of three months."

"Thank you for the math lesson. Three months seems a long time to wait to find out if I have breast cancer."

"If you'd rather, I can order an ultrasound."

"What good will that do?"

"It will tell if this is a cyst."

"Is that the same as fibrocystic disease?"

"No."

"But you don't think it's a cyst.

"Probably not."

"We already have a probably, Doctor Conger. I was hoping for a definitely."

"In that case, we could do a biopsy. That should answer the question. It's up to you, of course. But I really don't think it's much of—"

"I understand your thinking, Doctor Conger. I think we'll do the biopsy."

Doctor Cutterup did the biopsy. The report came back negative.

"So it is nothing after all," she said after I told her. "Thank goodness."

"Yes. We can be pretty sure now that old something is just nothing at all."

"*Pretty* sure?"

"Yup. Doctor Cutterup said he's practically positive he got it out."

"But he's not completely certain."

"It was a very small area we were talking about, and as there was no definite lump to feel, he had to go where he thought it was."

"You mean he guessed?"

"I would rather say it was an estimation."

"An estimation?"

"An educated estimation."

"I see. And how can I estimate the accuracy of his educated estimation?"

"I would suggest another mammogram."

"Very funny, Doctor Conger."

"I'm serious."

"Oh."

"We would get the mammogram to make sure that there's nothing there any more."

"No more of the nothing that wasn't there in the first place?"

"I don't want you worrying about this."

"I wasn't planning to."

"In that case you really don't have to do anything."

"It's up to me, I suppose?"

"Naturally."

"Doctor Conger, it seems to me that we're right back where we started."

"Not exactly, Ms. Sticklethwaite."

"You're right. We're not where we started at all. I'm two thousand dollars poorer, and the medical profession is two thousand richer."

"Two thousand dollars is a small price to pay for your peace of mind, Samantha."

"I had my peace of mind, Doctor Conger, until you took it away from me. I paid two thousand dollars to get it back."

"That's not fair!"

"It most certainly isn't. You suggested a mammogram. When I got one, you didn't know what to make of it. And now you want to do the same thing all over again. Do you know what I think about this whole business, Doctor Conger?"

"I can guess."

"Of the two ways of doing things."

"Yes, Ms. Sticklethwaite."

"This one is *every other.*"

Chapter 19

A Fitting Lesson

Dumster High School sits halfway up Hill Street just beyond the intersection with Maple. Built in 1923, it is constructed in the same fortress-like style as Dumster's three other architectural landmarks, the Talbot Building, the Block (currently operating under the alias of Abenaki Valley Heights), and the state prison. Of the three, Dumster High is closest in appearance and geography to the prison, which also resides on Hill Street three doors down. So closely do the two resemble each other, that for years the only real difference between them was that the prison had a brick wall and was a little shabbier looking, both of which distinctions, since being converted to a senior citizen housing project, it has relinquished to the school. It was not unusual, prior to the prison closing, for an out-of-town sheriff to march up the granite steps of the one and demand admission for his charge to the other. Such an event was occasion for considerable amusement among the inmates of the one, who were quick to respond with numerous witty remarks as to the officers having gotten the right idea but the wrong jail.

In the war between the forces of enlightenment and the forces of ignorance, Dumster High has been a fiercely contested battleground. Possession has passed back and forth between the two sides many times over the past seventy years. At present enlightenment prevails, but its hold is tenuous, and its army is in disarray. The current batch of recruits, despite the urging of their superior officers, are less than eager to take up the call to arms.

There are some fronts, the scientific and mathematical in particular, upon which they attack with zeal. On the historical flank they are more indifferent but with prodding are at least able to hold the line. However, when it comes to the literary—well, when it comes to the literary, quite simply—it doesn't. At the slightest whiff of an air poetic or a line fanciful, they dig into their trenches and refuse to budge an inch. Solid, stout, and utterly resistant to acquiring any knowledge that is not relevant either to the making of a thing or the use of it, they are constructed in mind of much the same stuff as the building they occupy. Bricks.

It was a fine spring morning as Samantha Sticklethwaite inspected the ranks. The faces of the troops before her were clean, bright eager faces. They displayed, without exception, that look of respectful attentiveness that clever schoolchildren develop in order to daydream at will without calling attention to themselves.

I suppose I should be grateful, she thought. It could be worse. They don't shoot up, and they don't shoot it out. They are basically good kids. Yes, that's what they are. Basic. Not that they're dumb. Lord knows these kids are bright enough—every bit as bright as the ones I had in Newton Center. Brighter in some ways, for they had, either by nature or by nurture—probably both—that unteachable ability to detect in a flash, the slightest whiff of falsehood. You couldn't put anything over on a Dumster kid. Especially not these, her senior Honors English class.

Hamlet was the day's battleground, and the room was pervaded with the heavy atmosphere that invariably accompanied the bard's presence. Trying to get some discussion started, she had asked Josh Brothers what he thought Shakespeare was trying to convey in his portrayal of the prince.

"Don't get stuck on yourself," he answered simply.

"Thank you, Josh. Now will you please read starting on page thirty-five."

With sullen reluctance, he took up the book. "To-be-or-not-to-be-that-is-the-question-whether—"

Mercilessly he rode over lines. Like a plow breaking ground, he trampled them underfoot with his endless dull monotone.

They never missed the point. It was the music they couldn't get. Their ability to mutilate the rhythm of the words was as uncanny as their aptitude for deciphering their meaning. Words were tools to them, no different from a chain saw or a tractor, and they would no more have thought of using them for mere pleasure than they would have thought of planting a cornfield in rosettes just to see how it looked.

Samantha Sticklethwaite loves words. What she loves about words is not so much what they say as how they *feel*. She loves the way they vibrate in her throat as they swell up from her lungs. She loves the way they taste as they swish around in her mouth. And she loves especially the titillating shiver she gets as they brush a farewell caress against her teeth before departing on their journey to the outside world. Samantha Sticklethwaite loves words with an actual physical love.

That Samantha Sticklethwaite has any love at all may come as a surprise to some, but the fact is, Samantha Sticklethwaite is a passionate person. And it is precisely in defense against this passion, a defense she has ample justification for mounting, that she has adopted the strict and proper face she presents to the outside world.

Samantha Sticklethwaite is always looking among her charges for kindred spirits. And every now and then, although after eighteen years she could count them on the fingers of her two hands, one comes along. One who had escaped the Dumster birthright of deadening practicality. At such times, Samantha Sticklethwaite will abandon her carefully constructed lesson plans, and, calling upon her chosen one again and again and again, indulge herself in a clandestine orgy of etymological pederasty.

If the good people of Dumster had any idea of what were the feelings that ran through Samantha Sticklethwaite as she listened to one of her favored few, they would have felt, if not actually shocked—for this is a tune not much played on the Dumster sensibilities—something akin to how they might feel if it snowed in July. A little surprise, a little curiosity, and a little displeasure, but not enough to make a fuss about.

The lesson on *Hamlet* ended, Samantha Sticklethwaite turned to word building. Word building, was, for the average Dumster High student, the essence of pointless drudgery. A set of awkward utterances never used in normal conversation and never seen in ordinary print, and which conveyed their point not one whit better than those with one fraction of the syllables. Word building stood, in their minds, accused, tried, and convicted of that one offense unforgivable to the Dumster social order—showing off.

"Chad, give me a sentence using the word eleemosynary." She called on one of the budding young curmudgeons in the back row.

Reluctantly the condemned stood to his feet. "The man who gave everything to the church was eleemosynary," grunted young Penstock, demonstrating both his knowledge of the word and his conviction that it had no place in *his* vocabulary.

"Elwin, will you try elucidated?"

"The teacher elucidated the lesson to the student," he replied, conscientiously parroting the example provided in the textbook.

"Nadya, egregious."

The child rose from her chair. As she did, her countenance changed. Her shoulders stooped, her hands began to tremble, and from her lips came the baritone voice of a middle aged man. As the ministerial tones reached her ears, Samantha Sticklethwaite closed her eyes. An involuntary smile crossed her face.

"Elegantly exhibiting an eclectic equipage of evanescent ecru," she began, heavily accenting each of the words in its turn, "the evangelical eminence expatiated expansively as he expostulated his elegiac eulogy."

Samantha Sticklethwaite's face screwed up, her eyes tightly closed. She began to sway rhythmically. It was almost as if someone who did not know that she was standing fully clothed in front of a group of children might think that what she was experiencing was—

"His effulgent ebullience was eloquent in its effusive echolalia."

The child droned on.

"But like some effervescent effluvium, it enigmatically evaporated as he embellished his exhortation with an exigency evocative of *egregiously* elevated egoists."

Samantha Sticklethwaite was transfixed. Her eyes open but unfocused, stared blankly at the class. Only her legs, quivering slightly, showed any sign of life.

"Elucidating yet engrossing, it was, if effusive, an estimable ecclesiastical encomium."

This concluded the recitation. The pupil sat down.

Although well there might have been at such a promiscuous display of verbiage, there was not a single snicker from the other students. Completely ignoring their classmate, all eyes were upon on the teacher.

The week before, Nadya had read, at her teacher's request, the death scene in *Romeo and Juliet,* and when she got to

Eyes look your last!

Arms take your last embrace! and lips, O you

The doors of breath, seal with a righteous kiss

A dateless bargain to engrossing death!

Samantha was thankful she had had the foresight to take a double dose of Ritalin. She hated her medicine. It made her feel so jittery, and it gave her such tremors that she had a hard time holding the chalk. She always took it before Honors English, but today, she had uncharacteristically forgotten.

The neurologist had told her that if she sensed an attack coming on, she could try to abort it by concentrating on something utterly commonplace—she usually picked unwashed dishes—and if the stimulus was mild enough it would work, but it was effective only to a point.

Samantha Sticklethwaite suffered from narcoleptic cataplexy, a rare condition in which the patient, under the influence of certain emotional stimuli will experience a sudden loss of consciousness. The particular stimulus may vary from person to person, but for any one individual it is highly reproducible. For some it can be a rush of anger. For others an attack of laughter. In a few instances, sexual arousal may be the precipitating factor. Such was the case with Samantha Sticklethwaite, and it was this distressing feature of her illness that some eighteen years ago had caused her to leave Newton Center and a young music teacher some eighteen years ago and that, by coming to Dumster, she had intended to bury, but instead had merely displaced. For there was, in her mind's eye, an all too great similarity between caresses softly delivered and words sweetly spoken.

"Derby dibsh," she mumbled. Then she was silent.

Ordinarily, Samantha Sticklethwaite would have issued some words of praise on the performance she had just heard, and although she did not now do so, it was not because she found the effort wanting. On the contrary, she found it to be extraordinary. And she would give the pupil her ultimate compliment.

Samantha Sticklethwaite fainted.

Chapter 20

Nadya

"Dad?"

"Yes?"

My short answer was intentional. I was involved in an important project and was in no mood for conversation, even with a beloved daughter.

Like most of those who have emigrated to Vermont from the city, I periodically feel a sense of isolation from the rest of the world and with it a need to stay in touch. This is not so much out of any real interest in such goings on, but rather due to an admixture of guilt and vanity—the former because I consider it my responsibility as an educated person to be *au courant,* and the latter because it somehow separates me from those who live here not because they choose to, but because it is where they were born.

Unfortunately, my years in Dumster have rendered me much enfeebled with respect to my ability to digest serious news. I am quite comfortable with the *Abenaki Mountain Times,* and when it comes to such issues as to whether the sanders or the salters should prevail in the great Rabbit Hill debate, or the pros and cons of extending the musket season, I am up to snuff on all nuances of the debate. I pale, however, before talk of an upheaval in Turkmenistan. Any mention of the leading economic indicators makes me actually sick to my stomach. Nonetheless, I have a duty to do, and I do it. Each Sunday I trundle down to Contremond's and, joining the throng of flatlanders gathered about anxiously awaiting its arrival, pick up my copy of the *New York Times.* For three weeks out of four, I just skim the headlines. Then I leave the paper lying conspicuously about, where it could be seen by any visitor who happens in. But on the first Sunday of each month, of which today was one, I sit down and read every single page of the damn thing.

Before Nadya's interruption, I was in the midst of an article discussing the end of the world. While such a subject is usually

found in journalism of a more jaundiced hue than the *Times,* I
had long since discovered what all devoted *Timesians* appreciate,
namely that the paper is not above stooping, under surreptitious
cover of science and health, to the more prurient interests of its
readers. The article was quite interesting.

Hoping to nip her nascent dialogue in the bud, I lowered the
paper just enough to expose my face and frowned severely.

"Are you getting addlepated, Dad?" asked Nadya, ignoring my glance.

"I beg your pardon."

"Are you getting absentminded? You know, senile. Or are you,
perhaps, bemused?"

"Bemused?"

"Preoccupied. Contemplating other matters. Distracted."

"I am aware of the meaning of the word, darling daughter. My
question was with respect to the nature of your inquiry."

"You forgot your pills today."

"My pills?"

"Oh dear! It's worse than I had contemplated. I am referring
to the pills you take so you won't have a heart attack. The one for
today is still in its compartment."

"Ah yes! Those pills. I'm sorry, my dear. I'm afraid I don't
think of them as *my* pills. And sometimes I do forget. Thank you
for reminding me."

"You are welcome."

I returned to the paper. There is this asteroid, Pericles by name,
which was last seen in our neighborhood some thousand years
ago, and was not expected to return for several millennia. But as a
result of a distant galactic disturbance, it has strayed from its assigned orbit and is soon to pass a mere one hundred thousand
miles from the earth, at which distance our gravitational force
would pull it into the atmosphere.

"Dad?"

"Yes, Nadya."

"What's in those pills?"

"I don't know."

"You don't know what's in them, but you're taking them anyway? Isn't that rather outlandish?

"It might be aspirin."

"Might be?"

"Or it might not."

"Just aspirin?"

"Yes—or not."

"Why are you taking aspirin or not?"

"I'm in a study."

"What kind of study?"

"To see if aspirin will prevent heart attacks."

"Is it working?"

"The preliminary results are encouraging."

"Oh." She paused for a minute, retreating into thought. Then she piped up. "Maybe Solomon should take aspirin."

"Why do you say that?"

"With his cholesterol being so high—it might be judicious."

"I don't think Solomon will get a heart attack."

"Oh."

Solomon was Nadya's baby. He was one week old, and his arrival had caused a considerable stir in the family. It was not at all something Trine and I had anticipated. Nadya's explanation that "Everyone else was doing it," was imperfectly consoling. However, it was a done thing, and we were determined to try and make the best of it.

Solomon was a most unusual baby. Round, smooth, and very white, he appeared to have closer ties to the Dumpty family than to the Bechs or the Congers. Under the circumstances, the resemblance was understandable. Solomon was an egg.

Solomon was a pleasant and well-behaved young egg. He had a perpetual smile, a cute little red nose that never ran, and two bright unblinking blue eyes. He slept in a bed made from a tea canister. I rather liked Solomon. He had a placid disposition, and he never raised his voice.

Solomon lived with us for two weeks. At the end of his stay Nadya took him back to school. We never saw Solomon again. Nadya never mentioned him either, except once at Easter when she said it was too bad Solomon was gone. He would have enjoyed the holiday, she thought.

Nadya took Solomon—excepting one night he spent on the windowsill when she had a social engagement—everywhere she went. She took him to classes. She took him shopping. She took him to flute lessons. She even took him on a skiing trip.

Curious about their relationship, I studied the pair closely during their time together. It was most instructive. I learned quite a lot about the raising of an egg.

134

If you break the egg on the first day, you can bring it back and get a new one.

If you are a single parent (which, for some reason I never determined, all of the students were required to be) it is not too difficult to get someone to take care of your egg. Even people who have never had eggs of their own are willing to watch it without complaint.

Having two or three or even four eggs is no more work than having one.

If you wrap it up tightly in Saran wrap, you can take an egg almost anywhere without the slightest difficulty.

No matter how fresh the egg is, you can take it to bed with you, and it will never wake you up.

If you forget the egg and leave it somewhere, even for several days, it will not suffer any ill effects whatsoever.

The only time an egg makes noise is when you drop it, and then it only cries once.

It's okay to keep all your eggs in one basket.

Boys and girls are equally skilled at taking care of eggs, but they do treat them differently. When boys have finished raising an egg, they tend to throw it against the wall. Girls are more secretive about the separation. Also girls make prettier baskets.

Egg grandparents don't have much to contribute in the raising of an egg.

I resumed my reading. There was hot debate about Pericles between the astronomers and the astrophysicists, two groups who never see eye to eye. On the inevitability of Pericles' arrival at least, both were agreed, as well as on the expected date, July 17, 2010, at 5:17 P.M. Eastern Daylight Time. But they parted company on the most important question.

"Dad."

"Yes, Nadya."

"I aspire to be a doctor."

"I think you would make an excellent doctor."

"Perhaps it would be prudent for me to take aspirin."

"I don't think that's necessary."

"Why not?"

"Women doctors aren't taking the pills."

"Are they harmful to women?"

"No."

"Women doctors don't want to take them?"

"It's not that they don't want to take the pills. They can't."

"Women doctors are not adept at taking pills?"

"The study is for men only."

"Why is that?"

"Heart attacks are a man's problem."

"Women don't get heart attacks?"

"Not as often as men."

"Don't you want to know if aspirin would help women?"

"That's why we're doing the study."

"But if women are not participants, how can you discern any benefit they might accrue?"

"If it helps men, it should help women too."

"You mean what's good for men is good for women?"

"There's a problem with including women in the study."

"What kind of problem?"

There aren't enough women doctors. And if you include both men and women, you need the same numbers of each. Otherwise you introduce bias. You know what bias is don't you?"

"That's when you discriminate against someone."

"Sort of."

"Why not just permit women who aren't doctors in the study?"

"That would introduce another bias. You need a homogeneous population."

"What about nurses?"

"Nurses?"

"Yes. Isn't there an abundance of women nurses?"

"Nurses in a study for doctors? I don't think so.

"Why not?"

"It—well, it just wouldn't work."

"Oh."

The astronomers, who tended toward the melodramatic, estimated Pericles to be about the size of Texas, and they predicted it would land with such an impact as immediately to parboil every living thing on the planet. The astrophysicists—

"Dad."

"Yes, Nadya."

"Could aspirin prevent breast cancer?"

"I don't think so."

"But you don't know."

"Not for sure."

"Has it ever been studied?"

"No."
"Does anything prevent breast cancer?"
"I don't know."
"Like a vitamin, or calcium, or maybe chocolate?"
"It's possible."
"Is anyone studying women to see if there is something that prevents breast cancer?"
"Not now."
"Oh."

Pooh-poohed this apocalyptic vision. Nonsense, they said. Pericles is not one jot bigger than Topeka, and when it lands, it's most likely to be in the ocean where it would be pretty harmless—except for the tidal waves. Of course they did concede that the heat generated as Pericles passed through the atmosphere would raise the mean temperature of the earth by at least twenty degrees, and that would eventually spell the end of all current life forms except earwigs and crabgrass.

"Dad?"
"Yes, Nadya."
"Are you indisposed to having a heart attack?"
"I suppose I am."
"Then you don't want to contract one."
"Of course not. No one wants to have a heart attack."
"Do you want to have cancer?"
"Heavens no!"
"What about a stroke?"
"No, not a stroke either."
"Then what is your inclination?"
"I'm afraid I don't understand what you mean."
"If you don't get a heart attack or cancer or a stroke, then you will have to get something won't you? I mean eventually..."
"Well—yes. I guess so."
"What's left?"
"That all depends."
"Depends on what?"
"Uh—it depends on—factors."
"What kind of factors."
"Oh, high blood pressure and cholesterol and diabetes, things like that."
"Suppose you don't have any factors."
"In that case—well, in that case you'd probably get Alzheimer's disease."

"What's that like?"

"It's not very nice. You get forgetful and confused, and someone has to take care of you. It's especially hard on families, because
they see the person they love isn't really that person anymore."

"It sounds rather distasteful."

"It is."

"I don't think I care to contract Alzheimer's disease."

"Nor do I."

"Oh."

The most interesting part of the story was how they figured this
all out. Nobody has ever seen Pericles, because the last time they came
through was about 255 AD, by which time the wise men were long gone
and people had their noses pretty much to the grindstone.

"Dad?"

"Yes, Nadya."

"When you have a heart attack, how do you die?"

"Most of the time the heart just stops."

"Like Grandpa?"

"Like Grandpa."

"Could the cessation occur when you are asleep?"

"That's when it usually happens."

"Oh."

It was based on a minor change in the orbit of some distant star,
which, the scientists determined, could only be explained by an unseen
visit from Pericles. From that they predicted when it would drop in.

"Dad?

"Yes?"

"I want to die of a heart attack."

"I see."

"Of the available options, it seems to me the most judicious."

"You have a point."

"Then why are you taking aspirin?"

"Maybe I'm not."

"But maybe you are."

"Maybe."

"It's a big chance to take. Is that circumspect?"

"Perhaps that's why I forget to take them. My subconscious is
looking after me."

"Oh."

It was really something. How they could foretell an event so
far in the future. They also predicted that, just before the crash—

"Dad?"

Chapter 21

Percival Chichester Winchester

"Humma, humma, humma."

Percival Chichester Winchester was feeling good. Sitting behind the wheel of his spanking-new red Corvette convertible he leaned back in the plush leather seat and surveyed the street before him. Lovingly, he stroked his mustache.

It was a magnificent mustache. A jet black handlebar of immense proportions. Percival Chichester Winchester's mustache was an object of admiration by all the women in Dumster, which they freely admitted. It was also an object of envy by most of the men, which they did not so freely admit, attempting to conceal it in muttered grumblings about his "puffing up," in their eyes an indiscretion of the highest order.

It was a warm and sunny day. Percival Chichester Winchester was attired in his favorite outfit. Matching tweed cap and jacket. Tan linen shirt open at the collar. Red cravat loosely tucked in at the neck. Plaid knickers. His favorite Meerschaum stuck in the corner of his mouth. Percival Chichester Winchester and Baby— the Corvette—had just been from Dumster to Rutland and back in one hour and twenty minutes flat. He stroked his baby smooth face and twinkled his baby blue eyes. Percival Chichester Winchester was feeling *very* good.

It had been a good day. Across the street, Winifred Best came out of Contremond's with a bag of groceries. Percival Chichester Winchester smiled. It was a *great* day. He touched the accelerator. Baby roared in response. Winifred looked up. Percival Chichester Winchester tipped his cap.

"Want a lift, Winnie?" he called out.

Winnie giggled, "Do I dare?"

In a single fluid motion Percival Chichester Winchester hopped out the car, opened the door, and waved her in.

"Do you dare not?"

Winnie crossed the street. She got into the car.

"My place or yours, baby?" He smiled broadly.

"Oh you, Perce." Winnie blushed.

Percival Chichester Winchester loved two things. Fast cars and pretty women. He had a way with both. He could take an ordinary car, and tinker with it and fuss over it, and, when he took it out on the road, could get a performance out of that car even the car didn't know it had.

As to women, some said it was the mustache, some the glint of his baby blue eyes. Whatever it was, they wanted it. He could be at a party, or at bingo, or in church, and he would look around with that big come-on-over smile, and hum his humma humma humma, and they would come a-running. Women hovered around Perce like bees on clover.

Perce had been to the altar four times. To each wife he had been a devoted and faithful husband, but when the marriage had ended—in each case because death did them part—Percival Chichester Winchester had come out of the blocks at full speed.

Percival Chichester Winchester took the same meticulous care of his own body that he did of his Baby's. "Doc," he said tapping his chest proudly when he came in for his last visit, "check this baby out! I got places to go, and I got people to see, and I don't want her quitting on me until I've been to all those places and seen all those people. I still got a lot of beans on my plate. So clean out my carburetor and tune up my valves. Put the meter to me and see how she runs. I want this baby humma humma humma!"

"But Perce," I said, "you don't need a checkup. Why at your—"

"Doc—" he warned raising his finger, "not a word. Not a word of it."

"I was merely trying to point out—"

"I know what you're trying to do Doc, and I appreciate it. I really do. But I told you before, and I'll tell you now. Not a word of it. Not one word."

He drew his fingers across his lips to indicate that the subject was closed. "Now," he said in a businesslike tone, "about that sludge in the fuel lines."

"Well, if you want to do it right, you should be down below two hundred."

"Two hundred! What's the story? Used to be three hundred. Then you told me two-forty."

"I know, Perce. But that was last year. We have new emission standards now."

"Gotcha!" he grinned. "Toughen 'em up. Good idea, Doc. Good for business too I bet," he winked. "Humma humma humma?"

It was *very* good for business. When things got a little slow in the department of patients coming in, all we had to do was cast our cholesterol nets a little wider, and the fish came spilling in. And although the official implementation date was not until 1996, I was thinking of racheting down to one-eighty now. Several of my colleagues had already jumped the gun.

But not for Perce. I could afford to be flexible with him. He was a steady customer.

"I suppose we could loosen it up a little, Perce. I mean—"

Perce shook his head. "Not a bit, Doc. Not a bit of it, I tell you. We do this strictly according to the book! I want this clunker humma humma humma. You say the word. I'll do the deed."

"Okay. Let's start with your diet."

"Oat bran, alfalfa sprouts and olive oil!"

"Can't do any better on that front. Exercise—" I looked at his sleek, trim body. "No. I don't think you need more exercise."

He grinned. "If I did, they might lock me up."

"Tobacco."

"Chucked the cigars last year, Doc. And the pipe is just for show." He slapped his hand proudly on his chest. "I'm pure as the driven slush now."

"So—" I said, ticking off the items on my list, "that leaves only one thing. Drugs."

"C'mon Doc! You know me better than that!"

"*Prescribed* drugs, Perce. I'm talking about medicine. To lower your cholesterol."

"STP huh?" he asked nodding. "Good idea, Doc. Sock it to me."

I put him on my favorite combo. Perce's cholesterol plummeted to one-thirty-seven, a feat he trumpeted around town to his great pleasure—and to mine as well. A healthy Perce was good press.

Cholesterol was the last thing on his mind now, as Perce popped Baby's clutch and took off with a squeal of tires. Winifred clutched at her hat.

"Well, Winnie, what's the answer?"

"Well, Perce, what's the question?"

"Can't you guess?"

"Can't you?"

Later that afternoon, Perce came barging into my office. "Emergency! Emergency!" he shouted at Maggie. "I got serious troubles, Maggie. If you don't get me to the Doc pronto, I'm like to bust a gasket."

She ushered him into a room. I saw him immediately.

"It's all over, Doc," he said despondently.

"It is?" I was surprised at this grim declaration. Looking dapper as ever, to outward appearances Perce seemed none the worse for wear.

"Yup. Done for. Finished. Kaput. I'm over the hill, and I might as well be six feet under."

"What's the matter?" I asked, concerned. Ever the optimist, I had never heard Perce talk like this. Something must be terribly wrong.

"The matter!" he exclaimed. "The matter? I'll tell you what's the matter. I couldn't do it. *That's* what's the matter."

"It?"

"It."

"Well, Perce, I would hardly say that's surprising. At—"

"Uh-Uh-Uh"

"Excuse me, I forgot. Please. Tell me what happened."

"Nothing."

"I understand. But I need to know the details."

He looked at me sheepishly. "It's, uh—personal, Doc. If you know what I mean. And kind of embarrassing."

"Come on, Perce—" I chided him gently. "Who am I?"

"I know, Doc. It's just that I'm not used to—I mean I don't usually—Oh hell! Guess you can't help me if I don't give you the whole scoop. But not a word of it to anyone, Doc. Not one word of it I tell you."

"Perce!"

"Sorry, Doc. I'm just a little touchy right now. Anyway, I picked up Winifred Best this afternoon. Took her for a ride. Well, that's when it happened."

"You mean when it *didn't* happen?"

"Yep."

"Right there. In the car?"

"Yeah, in the car!" he snapped peevishly. "Where else would we be? In the road?"

142

"I only mean that you and Winifred—in that car, that little car. I mean—Are you trying to tell me that you and she were trying to—"

"Right. We were trying to, but I couldn't."

"You couldn't—" I stopped. Even for me the subject was getting a little delicate.

Perce shifted awkwardly. "I couldn't find it!" He exploded with an anguished cry.

"You couldn't *find* it?"

"Not a bit of it. I tried. Lord knows I tried. I tried this way, and I tried that way. I turned every which way but upside down. It was no use. I just couldn't. In the end, Winnie had to do it for me. I don't need to tell you how that made me feel. Percival Chichester Winchester. Needing help from the woman!"

"I know it's difficult to talk about, Perce," I said speaking with some difficulty myself. "But I have to ask you this. Was it hard?"

"Oh it was hard all right. Every bit of it. Hard as a week old biscuit."

"Well that's something at least. If it's hard, it's a good sign."

"Is it?" he replied glumly. "Didn't do me much good."

"I only meant that if it's hard—that proves the nerves and the hormones are okay. Which means—but never mind the physiology. You say even though it was hard, you still couldn't—find it?"

"I told you, Doc, not a bit of it. Several times I thought I was close. But it was no cigar. You know what I think, Doc? I think I got that disease."

"What disease?"

"You know, the one where you can't—where I can't." He shook his head in frustration. "See? That's what I mean. I can't say it."

"Impotence?"

Perce burst into laughter. "Me, Percival Chichester Winchester? C'mon Doc. You gotta be kidding."

"But—I thought—you said—" I stumbled confusedly over my words. "You and Winnie—I mean you, anyway—couldn't—"

"Find my house? Well, I couldn't. And I'd still be driving around looking for it if it were up to me. My noggin, Doc." He tapped his skull several times. "It's shot. I got that—that Arm and Hammer's Disease."

"Alzheimer's Disease," I said smiling. Despite his discomfiture, I couldn't help it. "I don't think so, Perce. People often get lost. It's not necessarily a sign of Alzheimer's Disease."

"In my own town?"

"Anywhere. Especially if you were—distracted."

"Well I gotta know for sure, Doc. If the lights are going out on the dashboard, I ain't taking this baby out no more!" He struck himself forcefully on the chest. "It's off to the junkyard and on to scrap metal."

"Okay, Perce, It's easy enough to find out."

I put him through the paces. Dates, presidents, numbers, object recall. When I finished there was no doubt. It wasn't bad, but it was more than just absentmindedness. Painful as it was, I had to tell him.

"That's it," he said gloomily. "Finish me off. I don't care how. Just get it done. And be quick about it."

"You know I can't do that, Perce."

"I know, I know. Hypocritic Oath and all that. But here you been keeping me alive all these years, away from heart trouble and cancer and what all, and now, at my tender age, I'm coming down with the worst disease of all. You got to do *something,* Doc—please."

"Tender age or not, Perce. I can't keep you from getting Alzheimer's disease."

He looked me full in the face. "You tricked me," he said angrily.

"Tricked you? How?"

"All this time you been telling me, do this, don't do that, take this, get that—making me think that if I stayed healthy, I was going to live happily ever after. But I'm not. I'm going to die. And before I die I'm going to wind up in one of those places where life begins five minutes ago. And people will look at me and say, 'See that old coot. That's Percival Chichester Winchester. They say he used to have quite a way with his women and his cars.' Only they won't know what I *was.* They'll only know what I *am.* Which will be nothing. I don't want to die like that, Doc. I want to die right. While I still got the old humma humma humma. After all you done to get me this far, you got to finish the job. You owe me that!"

It was a most unusual request. But Percival Chichester Winchester was a most unusual patient. I was not about to do him in. But there was a way to help him out of his predicament.

"There is something, Perce," I said, "that should take care of you—quite nicely I think."

"Hit me up then, Doc," he said rolling up his sleeves, "and do your thing. I'm a ready to Say-o-na-ra."

"It's not something I'm going to give you, Perce. It's your cholesterol."

"I don't care a fig about my cholesterol, Doc. That's what got me in all this trouble in the first place.

"I know Perce. I'm not talking about getting it down, I'm talking about getting it *up*."

"Up?"

"Up, up, and away. Three hundred, four hundred, five hundred. The sky's the limit."

"I thought you said—"

"That was then. This is now."

"But what about the fuel lines? Won't they—"

"Pack it in, Perce. All you can. Get out the eggs and the bacon and the home fries—and be quick about it. Trust me. It's the only way."

Perce looked puzzled. "I don't get it, Doc. Must be the old light bulb is dimmer than I thought."

I explained my reasoning. Perce set to work with his usual gusto. Within three weeks his cholesterol had topped three-fifty.

"Keep it up fellow." I told him when I got the report.

"I'm on a roll, Doc," he said cheerily. "Watch me fly."

One month later he got to five hundred.

About two months after our last visit, Perce came down with a touch of the flu. Just a mild case I told him. Nothing to be alarmed about. But with his intestines on the blink, his gas gauge dropped. Then the kidneys gave out. The weakened kidneys put pressure on the heart, which couldn't take up the slack. Fuel supply to the brain fell off.

I see a lot of death in my line of work. Mostly I get used to it. But there are a times—when a sleeping infant stops breathing, when the wiring shorts out in an athlete's heart, when a tiny bubble bursts in a bright young brain—times when I have to check on the death certificate, under the part that reads "Manner of Death," the box marked "Untimely." Single flaws in an otherwise perfect body. Tiny flaws. Flaws that make me want to say. Take it back. Fix it. This body is still on warranty. But there is no warranty. There is no body back guarantee. And death has no sense of timeliness.

Then there was Perce.

One morning he was a little under the weather. That night he was dead. They found him slumped over Baby's wheel, a smile on his face and a pint of Ben and Jerry's on his lap. At autopsy every single one of his vessels was occluded. Brain, kidneys, heart, liver—all of them. Plugged so swiftly and so thoroughly and so—properly—that there could be no doubt, either to his loving family, his devoted admirers, or his useless physician.

They asked me to write his epitaph. I adapted it from Oliver Wendell Holmes's "Wonderful One Hoss Shay."

Perce was built in such a logical way.
He ran ninety-six years to a day.
And then of a sudden, he was struck.
And what do you think the doctor found,
When he got up and looked around?
Poor old Perce in a heap or mound,
As if he had been to the mill and ground!
You see, of course, if you're not a dunce,
How he went to pieces all at once,
All at once, and nothing first,
Just as bubbles do when they burst.
End of the wonderful Perce—okay.
Logic is logic. That's all we say.

Percival Chichester Winchester. If ever there was a timely death—

Chapter 22
Town Meeting

It was raining. It was a hard penetrating rain, a bone-chilling rain, the kind that takes a full blaze woodstove to drive away. It fell in great torrents, washing from the trees the remnants of winter snow that clung to the long shackled branches and staining what was left on the ground a dirty dull dishwater gray. Descending from the top of Hill Street, the rain gathered up the winter detritus and swept it down the gutters to Main. Now the size of a small stream, it charged onward until it reached the storm drain in front of Town Hall. There, depositing its load in great heaps upon the sidewalk, the unburdened waters plunged tumultuously into the sewers below, emerging eventually to be sucked into the teeming waters of the great river that, lusting for the fields on either side of its tethering banks, strained violently to break free.

Inside the building fell another rain. It was equally heavy, equally dull, and equally did it cast mud upon the waters.

It was March. It was the first Tuesday. It was ten o'clock in the morning. It was the day most sacred to all Vermonters. That one day of the year when the average citizen, rising above his ordinary sensible life, has the opportunity to make the same utter fool of himself as does the professional politician all the year long. It was town meeting day. Moderator Clyde Maxfield was presiding.

"Article Sixteen. Highway gravel. To see if the town will appropriate the sum of—"

"Mister Moderator," interrupted a hoarse voice from the audience.

"The chair recognizes Mister Purloin."

From the back of the room rose a small shriveled old man. Almost bent double by his kyphotic spine, his thin, scarecrowlike figure wavered unsteadily as he got to his feet. Steadying himself on the chair in front of him, he clutched a paper in his hand and waved it excitedly toward the podium.

"In regard to the reserved balance of the Luciah Webster Fund."

The words were bellowed out with a vigor that seemed to belie the frailty of the frame from which they emanated. The effort, however, proved the lie. Straining his fragile constitution beyond its limits, the speech propelled him into a violent fit of coughing which exhausted his energy. He collapsed back into his seat.

"In regard to the reserved balance of the Luciah Webster Fund," repeated the moderator.

This he did not out of any desire to ensure that all present had heard the question. Of that there could be no doubt. And even on the slight chance that someone had failed to hear the exact words, this particular speaker and this particular preamble had been such a familiar refrain at town meeting for the last decade, even had he not spoken them, any townsperson recalling the meeting later that day would be willing to swear on a stack of Bibles that he had heard Clarence Purloin address the matter of the reserved balance of the Luciah Webster Fund. It was repeated, rather, out of deference to the speaker, as it allowed him the requisite time to recover from his last sentence before he proceeded with the next.

"Which now stands at seventeen dollars and forty cents," Clarence screeched rising and falling again.

"Which now stands at seventeen dollars and forty cents," dutifully echoed the moderator.

"I would like to know—"

"Mr. Purloin would like to know."

"What has happened—"

"What has happened."

"To the balance of the previous year, which stood at forty-five dollars and twenty-two cents."

In his haste to finish this declaration, Clarence Purloin blurted out these last words at a velocity that exceeded his respiratory capacity. He was overcome by another paroxysm of coughing, during which he looked so poorly, that anyone not acquainted with Clarence Purloin at town meeting might have had legitimate cause for alarm. But all were, and therefore none did, and in time the fit passed, and Clyde Maxfield turned to Daniel Contremond, chairman of the Selectboard, and repeated the question in its entirety.

Daniel Contremond took the microphone. "As Mister Purloin knows, and as the good citizens of Dumster are, no doubt, aware as well—" he began in that ponderous tone so universal to political discourse that one might have thought he was a United States Senator instead of just the proprietor of Contremond's General Store. (Out of fairness to those who so conduct themselves day in and day out, I hasten to add that Mr. Contremond, although capable of donning the *persona politica*, is unable to wear it for more than a brief period, and it has been known that when Selectboard meetings have run too long, he has broken down and relapsed into plain speaking.)

"The Luciah Webster Fund was established in nineteen eighty-two by her beloved niece Marion Webster," he paused to nod in the direction of a sprightly old woman in the front row, who nodded politely in return, "in blessed memory of her aunt Luciah, Lord rest her soul. The fund, originally in a balance of two hundred dollars—a *most* generous sum—" another nod to the benefactress, "was to be spent at the discretion of the Luciah Webster Fund Committee, whose composition, according to the conditions of the bequest, shall be the same as that of the Selectboard, of which distinguished body I am honored, at present, to serve as member and—as chair." A bow to the audience. "The fund, according to the terms of the bequest, was to be used solely for the beautification of the memorial adjacent to the Dumster Town Hall."

"If you will please turn to page seventy-four of the town report, you will see that in the past year, the Committee has expended, for two flats of golden marigolds planted at the base of the memorial, four dollars and seven cents, to replace the bayberry bush which was killed over winter, thirteen dollars and twenty-five cents, and for cedar mulch—"

"Mister Moderator. Mister Moderator," gasped Clarence Purloin his face purple with irrepressible anger.

"If Chairman Contremond is finished—" Chairman Contremond *is* finished—"the chair will recognize Mister Purloin."

"I object!"

"Mister Purloin objects—"

"To such flagrant abuse—"

"To flagrant abuse."

"This town—" continued Clarence, who, buoyed by the superhuman determination of his indignation, was somehow able to continue speaking even though it seemed as if every last wisp of air had been squeezed out of him, "has—so—much—mulch—in every—yard. There is no need! It—is—a—disgrace! Let the record show—I object!"

149

"The chair thanks Mister Purloin for his observations on the Luciah Webster Fund," intoned Moderator Maxfield, "and the record will so note. If there are no further comments on Article Sixteen—There *are* no further comments on Article Sixteen—the chair will now move to Article Seventeen. To see if the town of Dumster shall vote to expend the sum of two hundred and twenty dollars to replace the street lamp on the corner of Hill Street and State Street. Such funds to be raised by taxes. The floor is open to questions."

Questions appeared from the floor. Answers came from the podium. Issues were raised. Clarifications were issued. And the agenda moved on. But Clarence Purloin was silent. Having carried on long beyond his abilities, he lay limp in his chair, black in the face and, to all appearance, lifeless.

In years gone by, there was never a cause too sacred, never a point too obscure, never an item too small, that at its introduction, Clarence Purloin would not be on his feet, objecting, reserving, demanding, whining, wheedling, and bullying, as if it were his personal responsibility to account for every penny spent by the town of Dumster. But too much time and too many cigarettes had taken their toll, and his lungs, once renowned for their disputatious prowess, could now rise but briefly to the occasion.

Eventually, under the assistance of his *aide-de-camp*, Young Lucien Persiflage, Clarence spluttered his way back to a tolerable state of animation. He tried to raise one more objection. But he failed. Clarence Purloin had run out of gas.

It was a bitter blow to a bitter man. A sad end to a great career. For the past thirty years Clarence Purloin had held undisputed claim to Vermont's most revered of public positions. Town contrarian. So well had he carried out his duties, so vigorous was he in fulfillment of the public trust, that there was much debate within Dumster as to whether his contrariness might actually be his preeminent virtue, opinion equally divided between those who favored it and those who held it to be the other of Clarence Purloin's matched set of merits—his parsimony.

Clarence Purloin had been, before ill health forced him to retire, Dumster's postmaster, and he brought to this position a degree of uncooperation remarkable even for the postal service. Clarence, who treated every piece of mail as a personal insult, considered any missive, destined from point A to point B, that completed said journey without hindrance, a blot upon his honor.

It was this capacity that I first encountered Clarence. I was still in Berkeley and needed to make arrangements for mail to be delivered to our new home while we traveled across the country. I called up the number given me for the Dumster Post Office.

"Well?" said a gruff voice at the other end.

"Is this the Dumster post office?"

"Ain't."

"I'm sorry. I was told this was the number for the post office."

"Nope."

"I need to talk to the postmaster. Do you know how I can get in touch with him?"

"Call home."

"Do you know that number?"

"Might."

"Could you tell me what it is, please?"

"4-3-6-2-1-5-4."

"Isn't that this number?"

"Is."

"Then I wonder if you could get a message to him at the post office?"

"Can't"

"Why not?"

"Ain't there."

"Do you know where is?"

"Might."

"Where is he?"

"Home."

"Could I speak to him please?"

"I'm he."

"Oh."

I explained my plight, adding, just for good measure, that I would be the new doctor in town.

"You get them doctor magazines?" the voice replied unimpressed.

"Yes."

"Other doctor stuff?"

"I do receive professional mail, if that's what you mean."

"Don't know."

"Excuse me?"

"Said *don't know!*"

"What is it you don't know?"

"Lot to put in one box."

"Well—I could have my magazines delivered directly to the hospital."

"Nope."

"I'm afraid I don't understand."

"I give you a box. You don't show up. I'm stuck with the mail."

"I'll show up. I've got a job, I've bought a home, and we're leaving today."

"Long trip."

"Yes it is. We're planning to take our time driving east."

"Don't."

"I beg your pardon?"

"Said *don't!*"

"Don't drive?"

"Nope."

"I really don't think that's any of your business."

"Is if you get kilt."

"I'm a careful driver."

"Nope."

"What do you mean, *no?*"

"Not less I see you first."

"Are you saying you won't give me a box until you see me in person?"

"Yup."

"But—What am I to do then?"

Silence.

"Excuse me, but I need to have my mail delivered somewhere. What would you suggest?"

A long pause. Finally, with great reluctance. "Could send it to general delivery."

"And you'd accept it?"

"Might."

"Thank you, Mister—"

"No magazines!"

"I won't forward any of my magazines."

Thus, delivered by one of its masters, ended my first lesson in the Dumster tongue.

I gave the forwarding address to the Berkeley post office, and, as it was cheaper than shipping them with the movers, I also sent our books by fourth class mail.

We took a month traveling cross country. When I arrived in Dumster I went straight to the post office.

The Dumster post office is located on the ground floor of the federal building. It is not very big. Twenty-five boxes just about fills it up.

"Didn't tell 'bout them books!" he snarled after I had introduced myself.

I had not forgotten my lesson.

"You didn't ask," I answered.

Clarence didn't talk to me for five years afterwards, and I am convinced it was his firm intent never to speak to me again. Circumstances, however, conspired to thwart him in this object.

It was a raw spring day. We had just finished Sunday dinner, and I was about to engage in a leisurely tête-à-tête with my cup of tea and the paper, when the phone rang.

"Doc?"

"Yes."

"Clarence Purloin."

"Good afternoon, Clarence."

"You need to see my old man."

"Is it urgent?"

"Nope."

As I was in no mood to go out, I suggested Clarence bring his father round the office first thing in the morning.

"Can't."

"In that case, suppose I plan to stop by after office hours in the evening. Would that be convenient?"

"Suit yourself."

"I'll be there a little after six. Tell me, what's your father's problem?"

"Dead."

Clarence Purloin lived on Main Street in one of Dumster's grand old houses, an artifact of bygone days when Dumster was one of the state's great towns, supporting both an active manufacturing trade and a thriving intellectual community. His grandfather had been a banker, his father a successful antique dealer. His ancestors had taken great pride in the house. Clarence was more humble.

The front of the house was almost completely concealed by a dense overgrowth of tall brush. Following a narrow footpath that I had to stoop to pass, I found my way to the front door, access to which was provided by a jumble of rocks piled on top of some rotting timbers. I knocked. After a while, Clarence opened the door. I encountered, upon entering the house, a great spiral staircase. It was designed, I assume, for the mundane purpose of providing access to and from the floor above. Now it played the more artistic role of a ceiling fixture, a transformation Clarence had accomplished by simply chopping it clean off about eight feet above the floor. This he had done to make room for a set of intended apartments, a project which had not met with any great success since Clarence had furnished them in the same style as his own quarters—sparse, and provided them with the same heat—sparser, and hot water—none, that he himself used.

Clarence lived in the back. There he had converted the kitchen, pantry and dining room into one large open room. In one corner was a grand piano, the only remaining evidence of ancestral glory. Covered with a long slab of plywood, it was now apparently a dining table. A smoldering stove gave off a vaguely familiar odor, which I could not place until Clarence explained to me that since his pipes had frozen, he had been obliged to use the incinerative method for disposing of certain waste products—products which were, he reminded me, an excellent source of fuel. Save a small mattress, virtually every other inch of floor space was covered with paper bags full of garbage. Clarence was in the habit of depositing these in the dumpster at the post office, but winter snows had rendered the going difficult, and he was biding his time until the way was easier. Clarence was a great believer in the biding of time.

I inquired about his father. Clarence directed me to the basement, where we entered a small cold cellar. There, slumped in one corner was an ancient looking version of Clarence. One glance was sufficient to tell me he had been dead for some time, but due to the preservative climate in the room, it was impossible for me to tell how long. I asked Clarence.

"Not too long."

"Could you be more specific, Clarence?" I needed something for the death certificate. "It doesn't have to be the exact. The time of day will do."

"Night."

"When did you find him?"

"Morning."

It was now two in the afternoon.

"Why didn't you call me when you found him down here?" I was puzzled by the delay.

"Didn't find him here."

"Who did?"

"No one."

"I'm afraid I don't understand."

"Died upstairs."

"And you carried him down here?"

Clarence shrugged. "Seemed the best place."

"You didn't have to put him anywhere. You could just have left him where he was and called me."

"Too early."

"What time was that?"

"'Bout ten."

"That's not particularly early."

"Too early to bury."

"He doesn't have to be buried right away, Clarence." I was getting exasperated by his unhelpful answers. "First he's got to be taken to the funeral home. Then—"

I know about that." he interrupted angrily. "I ain't dumb. The ground was froze."

"What do you mean?" It was mid-April, and spring was well on the way. "The ground's not frozen."

"Was in January."

Clarence's father had died some three months earlier. Wishing to avoid the cost of internment, Clarence had placed his father in this makeshift mausoleum until the soil was more suitable to a proper burial. Clarence didn't give it a second thought. He was just doing as he always did. Clarence was biding his time.

Chapter 23

Clarence Purloin

Articles were moved. Articles were passed. Winter highways and summer highways were proposed and seconded and approved, surviving, as they always did, a spate of amputating amendments from pretenders to the Purloin throne. They did not, however, emerge as whole cloth, for just as invariably as their approval signified the public's trust in its elected officials, so too did their modification prove the need of said public to remind those same officials of exactly who was serving whom, a need which, by mutual consent was sufficiently anticipated to permit a little trimming here and there without material effect on the provision of municipal services.

Finally the government of the people, by the people, and for the people, having completed its appointed task, repaired to the basement for dinner. There the fellowship of a communal meal quickly repaired the seemingly irreparable breaches of the previous hour, when the Comstocks had accused the Burkes of trying to destroy the town's character, and the Burkes had retorted that the Comstocks were such sticks-in-the-mud that had it been up to them, the town would still be without indoor plumbing.

While I was eating, Young Lucien Persiflage came up and tugged timidly at my sleeve.

Young Lucien was a lad of indeterminate age who had, for the last half dozen years, been inseparable from Clarence. Young Lucien had left school, by mutual consent, in the fourth grade, in which confines he had languished for many years. His mother had died when he was quite young, and Old Lucien, whose academic achievements were less than those of his son, had not done much in the way of supervising Young Lucien's education. Shortly after leaving school Young Lucien became Clarence's companion, running his errands, fixing his meals, and escorting him about town.

Soon Young Lucien became known as Purloin's boy. It was a title which Young Lucien held with great pride. Whether this was out of a sense of civic duty, or, as was often hinted around town, something altogether else, does not matter. The fact is that they were essential to each other. Without Lucien, Clarence would have been nothing. Without Clarence, Young Lucien was nobody.

"Doc." He spoke quietly, but there was urgency in his voice. "Cou'dya come to Clarence? He look pretty bad."

Pretty bad being the ordinary state of Clarence, I was not greatly alarmed by the news.

"I'll stop by this afternoon, Lucien," I replied and returned to my meal.

Young Lucien did not move. "Worse yet," he said softly.

Young Lucien was not an alarmist. A call of worst yet was not to be ignored. I got my bag and departed immediately.

Even for Clarence he looked awful. His color ranged from a deep purple around the lips, to pure ebony at the finger tips. His breathing was so labored that he had to grab onto Young Lucien's shoulders to steady himself as he gulped for air.

"I didn't—" he gasped hoarsely. "It weren't—I won't—"

"Be expected to pay." I finished, mercifully preserving the fiction that had existed between us ever since I had first ministered to him.

Regardless of how sick he was, it was never Clarence who went to the doctor, it was the doctor who came to Clarence. Although he did allow Young Lucien to notify me of that he was having trouble, Clarence himself never asked for my services. Thus my visit was, strictly speaking, not in the capacity of a professional visit, but rather a call which I made because I chose to. And any services I might provide, as Clarence had not requested them, could not be considered his financial responsibility.

Ministering to Clarence was a kind of public service, one which I accepted without complaint, as did Daniel Contremond who supplied the groceries he never sent for, Bill Comstock the wood he never wanted, and the town of Dumster the water he didn't need.

Clarence was thrifty. It was widely assumed that Clarence Purloin would just as soon let himself rot, starve, and freeze before he would pay his fair share of keeping himself alive. And probably he would have. No one knew. For no one had ever tried to find out. Thus Clarence depended on the inherent goodness in others, which, being completely devoid of such burden himself, he was that much better able to exploit, and he claimed, with some justification, that it was their pleasure and not his need which had made them do unto him that which he would never consider doing unto them in return.

"I—You—Don't!" he spluttered. Flecks of foam bubbled at his lips.

There was no time for socializing. "Clarence," I said firmly, "if I don't put you in the hospital immediately, you will die."

"I won't—don't have to—I got!" he screeched, waving his arms about wildly. He seemed to be trying to tell me something important, but I could make no sense of his incoherent speech. Most likely, I thought, the lack of oxygen had rendered him delirious.

Not so Young Lucien. Quickly grasping his master's intent, he went to the piano, picked up a set of papers, and brought them to Clarence. Clarence rummaged through them frantically until he found what he wanted. He pulled it out, and with a determined glare, thrust it in my hand.

I looked at the paper. Scribbled in Clarence's shaking hand, the contents were almost unintelligible. The title, however was plain enough.

Although otherwise quite undistinguished, patients do have one remarkable characteristic. It is a characteristic that, among the many varieties that constitute the human race, only the politicians also possess. They can hold, simultaneously and without the least difficulty, two absolutely contradictory points of view.

Ask a patient on Monday morning what is his greatest fear, and, assuming all to be well in his world, the patient will answer, without hesitation, to die. Come Tuesday morning, however, a touch of indisposition on the plate, and suddenly the life joyful has become an intolerable burden.

It is on days like these that patients can be found scurrying about with a most extraordinary thing in their clutches. It is called The Living Will. This document, flowery in language and eloquent in philosophy, espouses as inalienable, the right of said patient to achieve that very end which just so recently he had held to be totally abhorrent.

The end is a laudable one, and I support it wholeheartedly, adding only that it should not be undertaken without due consideration of what one's doctor might still have to offer, after which, if such measures have been fully exhausted, it becomes not only a right, but an obligation.

The Living Will states its premise boldly at the outset. "Death comes to us all," it says. It then continues on for some time in a similar vein before concluding as follows, "When the time comes that I have a terminal illness, I do not wish to be kept alive by artificial means or heroic measures."

All well and good. Three cheers, yo heave ho, and all that. But one man's terminal illness is another's temporary setback, and when it comes to heroic measures—well, I can understand that should a wild bear break into the hospital and attack one of my patients I would not be expected to risk life and limb trying to save him, but beyond that, things get a little murky.

I have discussed the issue with my wife. She is a lawyer but otherwise a fairly sensible person, and she said this. "The Living Will is like the Constitution. It can mean whatever you want it to."

I scrutinized the paper before me. With considerable effort, I eventually managed to decipher its scrawled contents.

"I'm gonna die. Nobody can stop me. Nobody better try. I don't want no help. I won't pay for it. I swear I won't."

Clarence Purloin's Living Will, like its creator, didn't beat around the bush. When his time was imminent, Clarence wanted none of my ministrations. This much was clear. On the other hand, Young Lucien would never have come without his master's tacit approval. Of that I could also be sure. Did he really want my help? Or was this merely the contrarian in him, determined to confound me one last time? I couldn't tell.

I had to find out.

"Clarence," I said, "do you want to die?"

Clarence shrugged.

Had he understood me? I repeated the question.

"Clarence. Do you want to die—*today?*"

He shrugged again.

"I can give you a shot." I spoke slowly and distinctly. I wanted no misunderstanding of my words. "It will make your breathing easier. It will put you to sleep. You won't wake up."

Clarence pointed to his Living Will.

"Twenty bucks," I said flatly. Clarence was a town institution, and I was not about to take responsibility for his demise. I had to be sure of his consent, and I could think of no better proof than a few of his closely held dollars.

Clarence shook his head violently. He had no intention of parting with a red cent, even for the peace he so dearly desired.

I took my bag and got up. At least, I thought, as I looked at him, the dull red glow of his eyes the only sign of life in a rapidly dying fire, with or without my help, it would not be long. Silently, I turned to the door and left.

The next time I was sent for, I thought as I walked slowly home, the assistance I would be asked to render to Clarence Purloin would not be of that of an earthly variety.

Chapter 24

Clarence Transformed

I had gone only a few steps when Young Lucien came running up behind me. "Doc," he shouted, grabbing frantically at my arm. "You gotta do somepin. It's owful!"

With Young Lucien tight to my side, hurrying me forward, I retraced my way back to the house.

Clarence was slumped over in the chair. His face grotesquely contorted, he gulped for air like a fish out of water. It *was* awful. I shook his shoulders.

"Clarence."

Clarence showed no sign of recognition. He was too preoccupied with his dying to be distracted by one of the living.

Suddenly, his eyes opened wide, and his pupils dilated in a fixed unseeing stare. A great whoosh of air, the last convulsion of a sinking ship, exploded from his lips. Then his deflated chest collapsed, and he lay still.

I turned away from the lifeless figure. "There's nothing I can do for him now, Lucien," I said quietly. "He's gone."

No sooner had I uttered my fatal pronouncement than Clarence, ever the contrarian, flopped over on his back, and, with his mouth twisted in a hideous grin, began to breathe again. This time, however, it was not the gasping respirations of the dying. It was the bird-like flutter of the dead. Soon enough it *would* be over. Soon enough.

One shot. That's all it would take. I reached into my bag, pulled out a vial of morphine, and drew it up. I jabbed the needle into his arm. Young Lucien looked at me eagerly.

"Gonna fix him?" he exclaimed excitedly, and shaking his master so violently I thought he would do him in on the spot, he cried in his ear. "Doc gonna fix ya! Gonna fix ya good."

I looked at Young Lucien. His face, brightly lit in anticipation of Clarence's resurrection, shone with the love he felt for this unlovable man. Perhaps Clarence no longer wanted his wretched life, but the boy surely did. Clarence had given me one order. Young Lucien an altogether different one. Which was I to obey? Whose choice was it? Whose life?

The legal world is exquisitely sensitive to the fact that life can be an ambiguous business. Thus, in setting forth a rule, it always allows one, provided one follows the proper procedure, to obviate said rule. This safety valve—loophole as it is often uncharitably called—is designed for precisely such instances as the one with which I was now faced. Where principle demanded that I do one thing, but desire asked for something else. Where the literal dictate of the law made, from the point of common sense, none whatsoever.

The remedy for the rule of the Living Will, is the Durable Power of Attorney. This convenient device allows any party of the second part, if so designated by a party of the first part, to act on said party's behalf in the instance where said party is unable to do so for said self—in short, to allow him to do what all who can exercise free will do on a regular basis, namely to ignore the best of our intentions.

Had Clarence properly given Young Lucien this authority, duly signed, sealed, and witness affixed thereto, my job would have been easy. There having been, however, no such formal delegation, I would have to take a more circuitous route to my end.

"Lucien," I said withdrawing the still full syringe, "has Clarence ever told you that if he were incapacitated, he would wish you to act on his behalf respecting his medical needs?"

Lucien's face was blank. I had fired the first round over his head. I redirected my sights and fired again.

"Have you ever done anything for Clarence?"

Lucien brightened. "Lots!" he said quickly.

"Good. Now I want you to listen carefully. Did you ever do anything for Clarence that he didn't actually ask you to do, but which you did because you knew he would want it done?"

For some time, Young Lucien screwed up his face in concentration. At last he slowly shook his head. "Doan noah," he said disparingly.

"That's okay. Let's try again. You've gone to the store for him?"

Young Lucien compressed his lips tightly. He was determined to get it right this time. "Shoah—" he said, "lots."

"And you bought things?"

"Shoah did."

"Did Clarence tell you what to buy?"

"Mostly."

"But not always?"

"Noo-aaah."

"So there were times when you bought something you knew he needed, like sugar maybe, even though Clarence didn't say to you, 'Lucien go to the store and get me a pound of sugar'?"

Young Lucien hesitated. He was unsure of the direction of my question and afraid that the wrong answer might get him in trouble.

"Don't worry," I said. "You can tell me. It's all right."

Young Lucien relaxed. "Shoah Doc. Lots times. Coffee too. An he doan complain. Least not much."

"Not much?"

"Noah."

There it was! For Young Lucien to be allowed to spend even a penny of Clarence Purloin's money on his own initiative, with *not much* the only complaint, was all the proof I needed.

"Lucien," I said looking him straight in the face. "Do you want Clarence to die?"

"Noah."

"Do you want me to leave him just as he is?"

"Noah!"

"You want me to do all I can to keep him alive?"

"Ayah."

"Even if that means taking him to the hospital against his wishes."

"Ayah!"

"And even though he will have to pay something for it."

"Ay-ahh!"

"Then, as you hold the Durable Power of Attorney for Clarence Purloin, I am obliged to act in accordance with your wishes."

Upon arrival at the hospital, Clarence was promptly drugged, tubed, wired, and whisked off to the intensive care unit.

Some time later I stopped by to see how he was doing. Sarah Trotter was there, puttering over his inert form. Engrossed in her task of restoration, she was oblivious to my arrival.

She had just finished the exterior work. Layers of accumulated grime had been peeled off. His tangled mess of hair was sheared to a respectable length. And his nails, of such prodigious length that they looked as if they could easily have, and in fact often did, serve as knife, fork, spoon, letter opener, comb, trowel, and a scad of other instruments less savory in function—those nails were now scrubbed to a shine and neatly trimmed.

Now she was checking the engine. She pumped up his pressure. She eased down his pulse. She turned his ventilator a smidgen here, and she adjusted his intravenous a tad there until Clarence was, in her eyes, satisfactorily tuned up and humming along. She swabbed his dry mouth, she toweled his wet brow, and, whenever he showed the slightest sign of agitation, she gave him an injection of a cloudy liquid that she called her milk of amnesia. From time to time she would step back from the bedside and cast upon her handiwork the appreciative eye of the master craftswoman before plunging back in to resume her labors.

Sarah Trotter was doing what she did best. Total care. Clarence, having been negligent in the custody of his body for the past seventy-odd years, had now surrendered it completely to her affectionate and competent hands.

That Clarence himself was insensible to his new state of dandification was probably just as well. The shock, had he been able to see his freshly exposed epidermis, now a color which had not graced his countenance since he was a bouncing baby, could well have succeeded in doing to the old reprobate, what his neglect had not.

"And how is our patient doing?" I asked, assuming my most collegial tone as I approached the bed.

"Just dandy!" chirruped Sarah.

I cast my doctoral eye upon the scene. "He may need, perhaps, a little more oxygen."

Sarah consulted a flashing light. "Ninety-eight percent."

"His respirations, however—"

"Are twelve."

I did my laying on of hands. "I think the temperature is a bit too high."

"Ninety-seven point three."

164

"And the pressure may a tad on the low side."

"One hundred and seventeen over eighty."

"His output is satisfactory?"

"Quite."

"And his input?"

"Matches to the milliliter."

There could be no doubt about it. Just dandy described Clarence Purloin to a T. So much so, that what I at first had feared might be either a very short battle or a very long one, now appeared to portend nothing more adventuresome than a stroll in the park.

"I would say we have him pretty well under control," I said.

"Under control."

"No complications as yet, it would seem."

"Not as yet."

"And none expected?"

"None."

"All signs are encouraging."

"Quite."

"Our prognosis is—"

"Excellent."

Our dialogue continued a bit along this vein. I inquired. Sarah answered, her response each time confirming what I suspected, and she knew, firstly that the patient was doing very well, and secondly that if nothing were altered, his chances of continuing to do so were quite good indeed.

While most of medicine is generally pretty flexible with respect to the business of diagnosis and treatment, allowing, without any real harm done, for one or the other to fall somewhat short of the mark, when it comes to the truly sick, there is no room for error. In such cases it is imperative that doctor and nurse work together in perfect harmony as each applies her respective skills to the task at hand. Part of this division of labor calls for the nurse to do the actual work that gets the patient better, and for the doctor to be more in charge of the overall situation, including, when any is to be given, the accepting of accolades from grateful patients and family. This is necessary because, without the doctor to advise, order, muddle, muck up, and otherwise interfere in every possible manner, the nurse's job would be so simple, that hardly any credit would attach to either party.

It was in pursuance of this end that I was obliged, at this point, to interject myself into the flow of things. As Clarence would have said, I had to piss on the tree.

I sidled over to the ventilator. Like a child in the candy store I longingly eyed the panel of glowing dials and flashing lights. Sarah watched me closely. A hint of alarm appeared upon her usually unruffled features.

"Yes-s—" I said looking thoughtful. "His respirations do seem satisfactory, although perhaps," I paused to apply my stethoscope to his chest as it rose and fell in perfect rhythm, "a little diminished on the left."

Sarah said nothing. Instinctively she moved toward Clarence.

I followed the first stethoscopic application with a second. "Yes," I repeated more authoritatively, "*most* definitely diminished on the left, and, I believe, a little excessive on the right."

With something of that mother-lion-protects-cub-in-the-face-of-danger pose, Sarah poised as my hand strayed first over the control panel and then to the tube in Clarence's throat.

"I think a slight reduction in the tidal volume, combined with two centimeters withdrawal of the endotracheal tube should fix him up quite nicely."

I proceeded to carry out my intentions.

For a few seconds nothing happened. Then Clarence erupted. With a monstrous cough, he sat bolt upright and turned a brilliant shade of scarlet. Sarah sprang to his side. In a single movement she laid him back down, returned the devices to their former settings, and gave him a hefty slug of her milk of amnesia. Peace having been restored, she turned to me with a look that was in every respect deferential and appreciative.

"Thank you so much, Doctor Conger. He looks much better now."

"Think nothing of it Sarah. That's what I am here for."

"Are you going to tea now?"

"I think I might—assuming that is, I am not needed here further."

"I think you have done all you can."

166

"If you have any problems—"

"I know where to get you."

"You know where to get me."

I started to leave. At the door I turned back. Clarence was doing so well. And I had done so little. It didn't seem right.

"Sarah?"

"Yes, Doctor Conger."

"He is doing very well."

"Very well, indeed, Doctor Conger."

"I anticipate that we will be able to get him off the ventilator soon."

"If you say so, Doctor Conger."

"Quite soon, I believe."

"That is encouraging."

"Perhaps tomorrow."

"Oh?"

"Perhaps sooner."

"Not before tea."

"No. Not before tea."

I went to tea. Shortly, Sarah joined me. We had a nice chat. She was very impressed with how nicely our patient was doing and was full of enthusiasm for my plan to get him going as soon as possible. Only it seemed a shame, she said, because he had been so uncomfortable when he came in, and now he was so perfectly peaceful.

After tea I went back to see Clarence. He was awake by this time but still under the influence of his soporific beverage. As is common in such a state, his activities fell into a certain repetitive pattern. He would tug randomly at his bedclothes, scratch his chin, look abstractedly about the room, and then close his eyes briefly until, responding to some unknown stimulus, he repeated the cycle.

Sarah moistened Clarence's lips with a wet cloth. As she did, they curled slightly upwards. The effect of this reflex action, although not of itself remarkable, was nonetheless striking. I'd wager my stethoscope it had never been seen by anyone save perhaps his mother, and that would have been a very long time ago. But there it was. Involuntarily or no, Clarence had smiled.

I didn't take Clarence off the ventilator that day. Nor the next. He remained in intensive care for three weeks. When he came out, I won't say he was exactly a changed man, for as his lungs recovered, so did his disposition, and soon he was demanding and whining and grousing away about every item under the sun. But his bark had lost its former bite. And his manner, unpleasant as it may have been, was not intolerably so. As if he were acting less out of true conviction than on the sense that this was what was expected of him.

One day I overheard him haranguing Sarah about one of the nurses, claiming that she was intentionally ignoring him and demanding that she be replaced. Sarah replied that he was right. Everyone, herself included, did their utmost to avoid coming into his room, and the reason was quite simply that he was a most disagreeable patient. If he wanted better service, she declared, he would benefit more from a change in attitude than a change in nurses. And he could begin by saying please when he wanted something and thank you when he got it.

Clarence, his eyes tightly shut during the whole of Sarah's speech, did not acknowledge her presence, but from that day forth, he could be heard—grudgingly and in a barely audible voice—to utter those very words she had suggested. He grimaced when he spoke them, but speak them he did. There could be no doubt about it. Clarence had mellowed.

Eventually he went home. He had been there only a few days when Young Lucien came to me. Clarence was bad again. I went over immediately. Clarence was lying on his couch.

"None of your damn fool questions, Doc," he screeched at me before I could speak. "Just put me in the hospital 'fore I croak."

I examined him quickly. His respirations were labored, but not drastically so. And his lungs, while wheezing up a storm, were still moving air. Clarence was sick. Very sick. But sick was Clarence' usual state, He was no worse than usual.

I told Clarence that his pace toward the inexorable, rather than showing any sign of quickening, seemed to be holding steady on the course.

"You won't have to go to the hospital, Clarence. An extra albuterol treatment should take care of the wheezing, and a few days of amoxicillin—"

"You don't know which side is up, Doc," he said angrily shaking his head. "Never did. Probably never will. I'm sick, I tell you. Sick! Sick! Sick!"

"Yes, Clarence, you are. But I don't think—"

"Shut your goddamn mouth. I know you don't think. You don't have to. Just get me a damn ambulance, and get me on that damn machine. And hop damn to it—'less the only traveling I'll be doin' will be in a box!"

"But Clarence, you don't need to be on the ventilator."

"Stop your damn drivel, goddamnit! I'm telling you what I *want*. That's all the *need* you need. So quit stalling. I'm not paying for your damn palaver!"

This was an unexpected turn of events. Here was Clarence Purloin, cantankerous old soul that he was, who would no more consider calling for my help short of imminent demise than he would think of offering to pay for such services, now doing both when he didn't need to do either.

Clarence Purloin had become a patient!

"That, Clarence," I said firmly,. "is something I will not do. There is considerable risk to putting you on the ventilator."

"Risk, shmisk!" he spat. You're all alike. Bloodthirsty vampires the lot of you. All you do is suck, suck, suck. Until there's nothing left. Nothing! Wouldn't it sour your cream to make a body feel good. Don't that just rot your day! Well let me tell you this, mister doctor man. The only time in my life I didn't feel like dried cat scat was when I was on that *risky* machine of yours. So get off your goddamn high horse and get me out of here, and be quick about it or I'll—I'll—I'll—" A coughing spasm interrupted him in the midst of his threat, and for a minute it appeared that Clarence might succeed in working himself into such a state as to make his demand justifiable.

I am as much a supporter of unnecessariness as the next chap. It is, after all, the stuff upon which my livelihood depends. Were I to limit myself to providing for my patients only that which was essential, I would long ago have been out on the street selling pencils. There is, however, a fine line, lightly drawn, and not very straight, but no less the definite, that a physician, in her eagerness to do for her patient, does not cross.

Should Clarence come in thinking he might have a touch of pneumonia and desirous of penicillin, it would be reasonable for me to comply with his request even if there were no evidence of anything more than a slight cold. The cold after all, might take a sudden turn for the worse. Or were he to visit Doctor Cutterup complaining of indigestion and ask the good surgeon to take a gander at his gallbladder, Cutterup would be permitted to oblige, whether or not the behavior of that worthy organ was much out of the ordinary. So be it. It was indigestion, and it was a gallbladder. But for me to prescribe digitalis in the first instance, or for Cutterup to remove a lung in the second—well, that would be beyond the pale.

In the ordinary case, to put someone with even barely adequate breathing on a ventilator would be over the line. But Clarence was not an ordinary case. Here was a man who had previously rejected my effort to save his life with a particular treament. Here was this same man, asking me for that very treament. And he *was* sick. And it *would* make him feel better.

Once Clarence needed the ventilator and didn't want it. Now Clarence called for one when it wasn't called for. It was a case of *quid pro quo.*

I called the ambulance.

Chapter 25
Change of Course

I am not a philosopher. Chicken and egg cases are quite beyond me, and angels on the head of a pin is a topic into which I have never much delved. On the river of life, I am a go-with-the-flow type of guy. I don't explore the tributaries, and I don't plumb the depths. In Berkeley I did wade around a bit in the tide pools, but the effort was unrewarding.

It may have been a sign of age, or maybe just a case of too much time on the hands—on which I will not speculate—but there I was one morning, having just completed the scrutiny of a stain above my desk, and having satisfied myself that it was the same stain it had been for the past ten years, about to inspect my teacup for anything of note in the dregs, when I found myself, to my surprise, ruminating.

The object? My recent experiences. First with Nadya, then Perce, and finally Clarence.

Clarence.

"Don't it just sour your cream," he had said, "to make a body feel good."

Ever since the first doctor gave, to the first patient's ailing stomach, a hefty slug of castor oil, and followed it up for good measure with a double dose of arsenic, the principle on which medicine has staked its success has been that if you want to get results, first, you bang the head against the wall.

How, if a patient did not suffer as a result of my ministrations, would he know that I had done anything? And how, without the relief that attends upon that suffering's abatement, would he know that he was better? Would he not be likely, as his condition remained in the state that conditions usually do, to feel that nothing had come of the effort? Pain. That was what told the patient he had gotten what he came for. Pain. That was the proof in the pudding. No pain, no gain. That was the way it always had been.

But, as I was learning fast, the way it always had been it was no more. Time after time have I found, upon making some particularly odious prescription to one of my patients, that instead of taking his medicine and bearing up like a good fellow, he has promptly trundled off to get a second opinion. Which would be okay with me, if only it were from a colleague in the flesh. All in the family after all. But he does not. Rather he chases after one of those pleasure pushers of the health care underworld who promise—with nothing more than a few vitamins, a couple of pin pricks, or a slap on the back—a quick and painless fix for all that ails. And when finally he does return to the fold—as they all do eventually—is it with repentant air to ask forgiveness? Heavens no! With defiant glee, the prodigal flaunts his indiscretion in my face and challenges me to match up.

Once such defections were only an irritating sore. But the sore was now a festering wound. Could I afford to ignore the challenge? The question was more than food for thought. It was bread and butter.

Turning from teacup to stain and back again, I sank into thought. Long I contemplated the stain. Hard I meditated upon the teacup. With the counsel of such estimable advisors, I came at last to the inescapable conclusion. It could hardly hurt, I saw, to substitute a smidgen of pleasure for a touch of pain. I would not, I vowed, abandon my principles. I would merely make them more palatable. In this manner I would be able to do greater good to a greater number of people. For what use was the true way if none were willing to follow it?

Thus, employing the common argument of those who wish to discard a precept that has been inconveniently weighing them down, but who have no desire to lose the sense of righteousness that prompted its adoption, I found myself in exactly the position I wished—that which would offer me the most possible gratification with the least possible guilt.

"Mr. Skittersly is on the line, Doctor Conger," said Maggie interrupting my reverie. "He says it's urgent."

In the ebb and flow of life, most patients, while enjoying the occasional high tides and suffering the periodic lows, by and large meander back and forth along the wide expanse of sand that lies in between, edging now closer to the one or easing now away from the other as inclination or fortune inclines. Accordingly, my contact with any particular member of patientdom is sporadic. There will, of course, be times when I am an intimate member of the family. But usually I am only the casual acquaintance. Slings and arrows or no, the ordinary being can brush his teeth in the morning and pick up his groceries in the afternoon without the advice and consolation of his beloved healer. The life of the average patient usually does not have very much to do with me.

Then there is Henry Skittersly.

When young Henry Skittersly was launched from shore onto that great sea from which there is no return, his parents, loving as they may have been, must have been distracted. Because they neglected to inspect their precious one's vessel to see if it was properly outfitted. And although the boat was a pretty one, and sturdy too, and although skipper Henry had a spanking new motor and the most darling of little uniforms, he was, unfortunately bereft of that most desirable of accouterments—a good set of oars.

So that when Henry at age forty-five, after a series of failures at marriage, parenting, employment, and virtually every other aspect of adult life, found himself, as it were, out of gas, he was, proverbially likewise, without a paddle.

Hopelessly adrift, Henry fell apart. Never much in the confidence department to begin with, he became a nervous wreck. The slightest noise sent him jumping for the chandeliers. The slightest setback put him in a tailspin. And the slightest malady—

Rather than bother you with the details of his medical record, which could suffice as material for several volumes on their own, let me simply summarize his most recent afflictions, so that we may proceed to the case at hand. In the last week, Henry Skittersly has suffered a stroke, pneumonia, two cancers, Lyme disease, hypoglycemia, and a yet to be discovered syndrome. In ordinary parlance, Henry Skittersly was a hypochondriac. To me he was a good customer.

"Good morning Henry," I said picking up the phone. "What's the trouble today?"

"My heart," cried a feeble voice at the other end.

"What about your heart?"

"Another attack, Doc. It's a bad one."

"I'm sorry to hear that." I said. "That makes three this week."

"Four," groaned the voice. "I didn't call you about the one last night."

"That was very considerate. But I've told you before—"

"I know, Doc. Couldn't get to the phone. Think it was a stroke too."

"That *is* too bad," I said sympathetically. "Did you take your pills?"

"Four reds and two of the long purples."

"How about that little yellow one I gave you?"

"Didn't dare. Last time I took it I got fibrositis."

"Perhaps you ought to come on in."

"Better call the ambulance, Doc. Can't make it on my own."

"Check your pulse, Henry."

"Already did. It's real fast. I think I'm in fibrillations."

"But you do have *a* pulse?"

There was a gurgling sound on the other end of the line.

"Henry?"

Silence.

"Henry!"

A loud thump. Then another. Then faintly, "Gaaawk."

"You still there Henry?"

The voice came back a whisper. "I'm doing CPR, Doc. The am—"

When Henry arrived, he was clutching at his chest. Sweat poured off him in buckets, and he was pale as a sheet of paper. Henry Skittersly looked just as one ought, if one was in the throes of impending cardiac arrest. But after a normal cardiogram, and a normal X ray, and a little sedation, and a lot of reassurance, Henry settled right back into his usual state of nervous exhaustion.

At this point it was customary for me to congratulate Henry on his prompt action, after which he would likewise me on mine. Then I would send him home with a new pill and the proclamation that all was well in the state of Skittersly. And until the next catastrophe, he would be secure in the knowledge that once again he had escaped the dread clutches. This time, however, I decided to take a different path.

"Henry," I said. "I'm going to put you in the hospital."

Henry staggered backward as if I had struck him. For a minute he was unable to speak. "Doc!" he gasped in a hoarse whisper when he finally found his voice, "Gimme a pill. Do tests. Do anything you want—only not the *hospital!*"

It may seem peculiar that someone so fond of medical attention would balk at an offer for admission to the one show in town where he could indulge himself to his heart's content, but it is not. Far from being paradise lost, to the hypochondriac a ticket to the hospital is a ticket to hell. For just as it is essential that his every hour to be consumed by terrors of the slightest twiddle, so too does he require the prompt resolution of said twiddle as proof that he may live to fear another day. To the hypochondriac, the hospital conjures up visions of irrevocable afflictions. To the hypochondriac, the hospital raises the specter of *real disease*.

"Yes, Henry, the hospital. But fear not. Things may not be as grim as they appear. In fact, I am actually quite optimistic about your prognosis."

Henry looked confused. "Wh-Whadya mean, Doc?" he stuttered.

By way of answer, Henry, let me ask you a question in return. Are you happy?"

Henry started at the question. "Happy?"

"Happy. Does life turn you on? Do you get up each day full of that old *joie de vivre*. Determined to go out and *carpe* the *diem* before the *diem carpes* you?"

"Well," he said sheepishly. "First thing I usually do when I get up is go for a jog."

"Excellent. A worthy activity. The body is temple of the mind. Do you *like* to jog?"

"Do I like to jog?" he laughed harshly. "Are you crazy?"

"Perhaps. Let me ask you this. Why do you do it?"

"Why?" Henry said, puzzled. "Because *you* told me to, Doc. It's good for me. It keeps me—"

"Healthy?"

"Yeah. Well, sorta. I mean, healthier than I would be at least. Don't I look healthy? For me?"

"The very picture."

"It isn't easy, you know."

"A constant struggle."

"There's a lot of bad stuff out there."

"Boggles the mind."

"But I never give up."

"Semper fidelis."

"Although—"

"There's a rub."

"Sometimes I wonder—"

"If—"

"If."

Henry stared at the wall.

"Henry."

"Huh?"

"Does it make you happy?"

"Does what make me happy?"

"Being healthy."

"Does being healthy make me happy? What kind of question is that, Doc? Healthy has nothing to do with happy."

"Forgive me, Henry, I misspoke. Forget that I asked. Let's discuss your colonoscopy."

"That was your idea too," he said with some irritation. "You said it was the best way to detect colon cancer. And it *was!* They found a polyp. Practically cancer, Doc Robertson said. Woulda been if I'd waited any longer."

"Are you glad about that?"

"Of course! I don't want to get colon cancer."

"No. I'm sure you don't. So you'll have another one—"

"Next year. That's what Doctor Robertson recommended. Just to be safe."

"Quite. And you've managed to get your cholesterol down to one hundred and twenty-five. That's quite an accomplishment."

Henry beamed. "Yes," he said proudly. *"That* was hard work."

"It is tough."

"Tough isn't the word. You know how you made me put down that list of all the foods I like. And post it up on the refrigerator. And then—"

"I know."

"Which got it down to one-eighty. You said that shoulda been okay. But—"

"That was too bad about the HDL."

"You're telling me. My cousin's cholesterol is over three hundred. He practically lives at McDonald's, but his HDL protects him. I don't hold it against him. It's just—"

"You envy him a little?"

Henry sighed, "You know when I miss it the most?" He lowered his voice to a whisper. "At night, after a tough day, and I'm sitting down with a good book and I get that urge—"

"Chocolate Chip Cookie Dough?"

"New York Super Fudge Chunk. But that's the price—And those pills! Ooeey! They ought to offer those babies with a mortgage!"

"And a good investment they are, Henry. Even your blood pressure is better."

"Thanks to Lopressor."

"All in all, you should be quite pleased with the state of the Skittersly."

"Oh, I am," he said nodding. "I only wish—" He stopped.

"I know, Henry. But impotence is a small price to pay for good health."

"I'm not complaining, Doc." he said quickly. "I mean—I don't want to have any more heart attacks. Not any more than I have to anyway."

"Or cancers either."

"God, no!"

"So. Let's see. You don't want to get heart attacks, or cancers—"

"Or strokes, Doc. Don't forget them."

"Or strokes. Tell me, Henry, what *do* you want to get?"

"What do I *want* to get?"

"What is your disease of choice? Your favorite? The one you like the best. The one you want to die from."

"Henry flushed. "What do you mean, Doc? I don't want to die of anything!"

"Which is why you do all this."

"Henry stiffened angrily. "Do you think I'm doing it for fun?"

"Not at all. But suppose—just suppose. That you could get the same results that you are working for now. That you could wind up in *exactly the same position,* and that you could do it without jogging, without diets, without colonoscopies—without even drugs. What would you say to that?"

Henry looked at me suspiciously. "Are you pulling my leg, Doc? 'Cause if you are—"

"I'm quite serious, Henry. Very serious. *Dead* serious! Chuck it all. The whole lot. Would you like that?"

"Uh—Sure! I'd love it. I'd be—"

"Happy?"

"Happy as a—but you're talking pie in the sky, Doc. I can't do that."

"Sure you can. It's easy. All you have to do is *just say no.*"

"But—"

"Listen, Henry, Here's the Truth about prevention. It's an illusion. A fraud. A scam. Because no matter how careful you are, no matter how many pills you take, the end is still the end. Everybody dies.

"What does that mean? Your demise, if it does not come from one disease, will come from another. And if by careful effort you have managed to escape everything from A to Y, when that end eventually comes, it will be at the hands of Z.

"Life, Henry, is a zero sum game. So if you keep on the way you are now, you're going to live a ripe old age. And then—*you'll keep on living!* Until you get the only disease that's left. Alzheimer's disease. Believe me, you don't want Alzheimer's."

"But it's not too late. If you act now, you still have a chance to change your fate. My recommendation—a heart attack. One minute you're feeling fit as a fiddle and the next—you're pushing up daisies. Lung cancer isn't so bad either. Why compared with—"

"That's enough, Doc," Henry said quietly. "I get the picture."

"So what do you say? Is it forget about tomorrow and live for the moment? Or are you going to keep on making yourself a slave to an illusion of immortality?"

Henry hesitated. "Why are you telling *me* this, Doc?" he asked uncertainly. "I mean, don't take this wrong, but when it comes to cutting off the nose to spite the face, that's not usually your line of work."

"My only interest is your welfare."

"But if I stop everything I'm doing. If I ignore my symptoms— If you don't treat my—you're not planning to drop me, are you Doc?" A note of panic crept into his voice. "You wouldn't do that!"

"Of course not. Remember—I want to bring you into the hospital."

"But if you're not going to do anything to me—"

"Not *to* you, Henry, *for* you!"

"For me?

"For you!"

"But I don't feel bad. I mean, not *that* bad anyway. At least not now."

"I'm not talking about feeling bad, Henry. I'm talking about feeling *good.* "

Henry laughed, "By going into the hospital? That's a good one, Doc."

"I mean it Henry. You are skeptical, and you have every right to be. But there's no reason going to a doctor shouldn't make you feel good. Just like going to the chiropractor"

Henry stared at me for a long time without replying. Finally he spoke cautiously. "You're practicing now, Doc. That's what you're doing, isn't it?"

"Of course I'm practicing, Henry. That's what a doctor does."

"I don't mean that kind of practicing, Doc. I mean the other kind."

"What other kind?"

"For a book. Working up some of that weird stuff that you like to put in."

"I am not doing this for a book, Henry," I said. "I'm doing it for you."

Henry was silent.

"Henry, do you remember what I asked you a minute ago?"

"About coming into the hospital?"

"About being happy."

"Oh, that."

"Well?"

"Well, I'm—pretty happy."

Pretty happy?"

"Sort of."

"How are things at work?"

"Slow."

Henry worked at Acme Tool and Die, which had fallen on hard times. They had just laid off twenty workers, and prospects for the future were bleak.

"And the divorce?"

"Six months, the lawyer says."

"The Valium I gave you last week. Is it helping?"

"I guess. But I'm under a lot of stress right now, Doc. It takes its toll."

"Makes you feel run down."

"Yeah."

"Like you just can't get a grip on things."

"Um huh."

"And you're losing control."

"You said it."

"But if you could just take a break—step back from it all for a little breather, you know you could work it all out."

"I've been thinking about a vacation."

"But where could you go? And what would you do? And wouldn't you be trying so hard to relax that it would wind up worse than if you never went?"

"That's a nail on the head."

"You'd like not to have to think about it."

"Wouldn't I ever!"

"In fact, what you'd really like is not to have to think anything—not one blessed thing."

"Sure would. But where can I do that and still wake up in the morning?"

"In the hospital."

"Henry looked at me blankly.

"Here's the deal. You come in. We put you to bed. We tuck you in at night. We get you up in the morning. We feed you, we wash you, we clothe you. When you're sad we give you pep-uppers.

When you can't sleep we give you lay-downers. We do it all. You don't have to do a blessed thing."

"But Doc—you just said I'm not sick."

"Sick, schmick. This is about *well!* I can even give you something to paralyze your muscles. We're talking *total* relaxation!"

"How could I—"

"Breathe? You won't have to. We'll even do that for you."

"Hold it, Doc. You're not putting me on any breathing machine!"

"Suit yourself. The point here is total stress reduction. Tailor made to Henry Skittersly. You'll come out of this feeling like a new man. I promise you."

"I—don't know, Doc. It sounds kind of iffy. I mean, I might catch something. People *die* in the hospital, you know!"

"Yes, Henry. But those people are *diseased.* And the stuff we do for them—it's all wasted, because they're too sick to appreciate it. But not you, Henry. You'll love it. Come on, give it a try. What have you got to lose?"

"Well—"

"Well!"

"If you really think it will work."

"It's a guarantee."

"I sure could use a leg up."

"I'll give you two."

"Maybe—maybe I'd better ask my therapist. Not that I don't trust you, Doc. It's just—"

"It's not me we're talking about, Henry. It's you! *You've* got to be in charge. Not me, not your therapist, not nobody else but you, Henry Skittersly!"

Henry sighed heavily. "All right. I'll give it a try. How about next week?"

"Not next week, Henry. Now."

"*Now?* I can't do it *now!* I got things to take care of. Tomorrow. I'll come in tomorrow."

It was a feeble attempt to wriggle out. But he was hooked. And I wasn't going to let him get away.

"Now is now, Henry," I said handing him a set of papers. "Your orders are written, and the bed is waiting. Come on in, the water's fine."

Chapter 26
Dean Cabot Cabot

It had not been an good year for Dean Cabot Cabot.

There was a time when he stood proudly at the helm of his boat, revered leader of the starship of the academic fleet. There was a time when all he had to do was make a wish, and it was granted. There was a time when nothing was too good for the medical school.

That time was past.

It wasn't fair, he thought bitterly sitting behind his desk and looking out over the wide expanse of his office. It just wasn't fair. Here he was, leading the charge against death and disease. Here he was, showing the world the promise of a glorious tomorrow. Here he was, dedicating his life to the welfare of others. And what was he getting for all this in return? Nothing but abuse!

Had he not fulfilled his obligations? Had he not executed his charges? The record spoke for itself. He and his colleagues had built machines that could look into parts of the body whose existence wasn't even dreamed in days gone by. He and his colleagues could take organs once considered hopelessly beyond repair and fix them with perfectly functioning replacements. He and his colleagues had drugs that could stop a heart attack in midstream, kill malignant cells on the spot, remove sludge from aging vessels. They even had a drug that would grow hair! Smallpox was a disease of the past. Soon too would be sickle cell anemia and cystic fibrosis. Heart disease was on the run. Cancer not far behind. He had promised, and he had delivered. Medicine had done itself proud.

But where were the accolades of a grateful public? Nowhere that he could hear. Where were the students eager to become the healers of tomorrow? No place he could see. And where was the money to support medicine on its inexorable march towards immortality? Not in his pockets.

On all sides they were beating on the walls, trying to tear down the castle he had worked so hard to build. Too much! they cried. Too extravagant! they claimed. Unnecessary! they charged.

Hah! He allowed himself a bitter smile. Unnecessary indeed! Unnecessary that is until it came to their own welfare, and then— even the sky wasn't high enough for these self-righteous whiners. Fools. Imbeciles, the whole damn lot of them.

Where would they rather spend their money? On investment for the future they claimed. But what better investment for our country's future than an army of well-equipped and well-trained doctors? And what better places to invest in than the schools needed to train them properly? And who better to trust to do that training than—but there they were—businessmen, politicians— yes, even patients—grousing about the cost of medicine, a mere fourteen percent of the GNP, a paltry $950 billion. Nickel-and-dimers they were, a sorry bunch who wouldn't know what was good for them if it smacked them in the face, which, despite himself, he had more than half a mind to do.

It wasn't just the money. People had a tendency to act out now and then. Especially about money. This was only natural. He understood, and he forgave. It was the lack of appreciation that really stuck in his craw. It was the damned ingratitude that just made him sick.

Dean Cabot Cabot was one of those unfortunate souls who never should have been assigned to the twentieth century. Possessed of a great sense of honor, but not much overburdened either with perseverance or ambition, he would have been better suited to have served as the governor of some impoverished Anglo-Saxon colony, where he could have been assured an ample supply of the unquestioning reverence he so greatly needed. Perhaps in tacit recognition of this, the dean had chosen a career which seemed to be the best available approximation of such a post. He had no way of knowing how much the times would change it.

It was hard not to commiserate. Here was a man so accustomed to appreciation, now being subject to ridicule. Here was a man who just wanted to be generally admired as a marvelous fellow being called, as one wag wrote of him and his cohorts, "perhaps the greatest collection of pompous swindlers since royalty was replaced by constitutional government."

Dean Cabot Cabot was not a selfish man. He had no need to be. The cumulative efforts of seven generations of Cabots before him had accumulated sufficient stock of wealth and stature that the dean could afford to squander a little. He was proud that he had chosen the path of self-sacrifice, and, despite the grumbling of some curmudgeonly uncles, who could see—excepting an occasional ambassadorship for those Cabots completely bereft of business sense—no life beyond the family business, First Bank of Boston, his career had been, if not approved, at least tolerated by the rest of the clan.

But gray sheep or no, Dean Cabot Cabot was not unmindful of the station in which his name placed him. Neither was he without a sense that, for the path he had chosen, he was entitled to appreciation from pretty much everybody. And now, to be rebuked at every turn, to have his every step, yes, even his motives, questioned. It was too much. He was hurt. He was sorely hurt.

Dean Cabot Cabot was a sensitive man.

The dean and I had been classmates both in college and in medical school. And although actual friendship I would not presume to claim, we were on friendly terms. He was at heart a good fellow, and I liked him. He, in return, tolerated me. And when our careers wound us up in the same neck of the woods, even though he nested in the uppermost branches of the highest tree, while I had settled in a lowly burrow, we maintained the relationship of our younger years, although it now consisted wholly in his inviting me once a year to lunch with him at the faculty club, where we would chat about old times. I felt honored that he would condescend to me. He felt gracious in his condescension. We both knew the limits of our relationship and so, although it did not grow during the years I had been in Dumster, it did survive.

It was, therefore, with no little surprise that he greeted me when I called to propose a meeting. It was a significant deviation from protocol, and although he was cordial, his tone conveyed his awareness of the deviation, as well as an uncertainty that it was entirely proper. Nonetheless, he readily consented, and we set a date for the following week.

"Good to see you again, Beach," he greeted me with the effortless hale-fellow-well-met graciousness so natural to one who is in the habit of hailing well-met fellows every day. "It seems like only yesterday we saw each other last."

"Yes," I agreed. "Three months must seem hardly a day to one living at your pace. I don't know how you keep it up. Especially the way things are today."

The dean gave a heavy sigh. "It *is* a burden," he said.

"But you bear up well, Cab," I said sympathetically. Bearing up was the highest form of flattery he could receive, and I wanted to lather him with a hefty slug before I approached the subject I had in mind.

"Perhaps," he conceded, "but it exacts its price."

"A terrible toll."

"It's no picnic, you know."

"Far from it."

"Wouldn't wish it on my own worst enemy."

"Don't know any other who could stand it."

"I suppose not."

"It's not for the meek of heart."

"No indeed."

"I do my best."

"And none could do better."

He sighed a more satisfied sigh. My point had been well taken.

"I see from the papers that you've been down to Washington trying to knock some sense into those Huns. Now there's a thankless task."

"You said it there," he assented, shaking his head. "Talk about missing the boat. Those fuddleheaded mugwumps aren't even in the right ocean. Do you know what they want me to do? Do you have any idea?"

Although I knew perfectly well, since both the medical journals and lay press had been full of nothing else for the last three months, I thought it proper to allow him to enlighten me. I indicated in the negative.

"They want to destroy us, that's what! Ruin everything. They'll take us back to the stone age. Why if old Abe Flexner were alive today, he'd have a stroke. It's horrible. It's terrible. It's—It's—"

He stopped, too full of emotion to speak.

The Flexner Report, issued in 1910, found that of the one hundred and fifty-five medical schools in the country, only one, Johns Hopkins, provided an education based on the principle that medicine was a science. The report led to a complete restructuring of medical education. It was, as I well knew, but the dean could never begin to comprehend, on the whole a mixed blessing. For the undeniable advantage of quackery as a medical philosophy is that it breeds in the patient, a level of expectation of reaching cure commensurate with the physician's skill in providing one.

"Do you know what they want to do?" he spluttered angrily. They want to turn us all into—G-G-G—"

"GP's?" I finished, mercifully supplying the word he was unable to utter. General practitioners were, within medical education circles, a category of fish too unsavory even to mention. Although necessary to perform the profession's dirty work, they were beneath all dignity. Inside the dean's hallowed halls, general practitioners were never spoken of. They simply did not exist.

In this fiction I am an internist, the title applied when I started out, to those of us who ply our trade on the dubious fringe. My younger counterparts stake their claim as family practitioners. Nobody ever admitted to the G-word.

"It's preposterous!" he exploded. "Why, those ninnies had the nerve to tell me that the whole *problem* with medicine these days is that we have too much specialization. Too many doctors. And, I quote, 'who care more for their diseases than their patients.' One of them even said that it was *my* fault."

"Yours?"

"Can you imagine that?" he exclaimed indignantly. "He claimed we have intentionally raised the cost of medical education so high that students are forced to seek high-paying specialties in order to repay their debts. I'll tell you what our *problem* is. We've gotten too good at keeping alive dunderheads like them!"

"Forget about the dunderheads, Cab. When it comes to the bottom line, we've got what the people want."

"That's right!" he said pounding his fist on the table. "We've got their health."

"And their happiness."

"And their happiness." he echoed vaguely.

"As always, Cab, you have hit the nail right on the head. And that's what I wanted to talk to you about. I have an idea—it's only a germ of a thing—about how we can turn things around. It has to do with patients."

"Patients?" He was puzzled. Patients were not a commodity with which Dean Cabot Cabot ordinarily had much traffic. Although he was aware of their theoretical value to the profession, he had no feeling for what they actually were.

"Patients," I said. "Many of whom are voters."

He perked up at the mention of this more familiar constituency.

"Well yes—quite—indeed! But I am not sure—"

"How it helps. As usual, you are being overly modest. The patient is the spearhead of medicine—you told me that once. And I've never forgotten it." Although the dean had never spoken these actual words, I thought it advisable to take this tact in preparing him for what I had to suggest. Like most sensitive people, Dean Cabot Cabot took best to ideas that he considered of his own creation.

"That's what made me think—that we—you, I mean—could use patients to help get things back to the way it used to be."

"Used to be," he sighed wistfully.

"And could be again."

"Could?" He looked doubtful.

"With your leadership. Patients and doctors are natural allies. We've just lost touch with each other. All we have to do is get them back in the fold, and we're in the pink. Politicians may get high and mighty, but if patients take up our cause, those blockheads will be like putty in our hands. What I was thinking was—"

I stopped. The dean, who had twice stifled a yawn, was now looking at his watch. I had lost the moment. But I had been so close. I was determined to give it another try.

"I know it's getting late," I said hurriedly. "I don't want to keep you. Why don't you drop by to see me sometime. You'll get a better sense of what I'm talking about if you see it in action. Besides, it would do you good to get out of this ivory tower. Come see how the other ninety percent lives."

There was a long silence. "Well—" he said doubtfully. "I don't know—" Suddenly he perked up. "Wait—Why not? Why not indeed! Actually, Beach my boy, your suggestion may be quite timely. Yes, I'd love to come down. It would do me good. Get my finger back on the pulse of medicine. How about next Tuesday at eight? In Danville? Would that be convenient?"

"In Dumster would be fine," I said elated. "It would be most convenient indeed."

Chapter 27

The Visit

Mrs. Lawrence P. Rothweiler III was not well. A vague malaise had come over her, and her ordinarily optimistic disposition had vanished. Her joints ached when she got up in the morning. Her stomach growled if she tried to eat lobster. Going downstairs, her legs wobbled like rubber. Her memory was failing, likewise her energy. Worst of all, her skin—her beautifully smooth, refurbished epidermis—had developed, almost overnight, wrinkles the size of the Grand Canyon. Mrs. Rothweiler was falling apart.

She mentioned her troubles to Dean Cabot Cabot. He was a family friend. The dean, correctly making the diagnosis all too common to those of Mrs. Rothweiler's class—the condition of too many years spent and not enough appreciation to show for it—suggested as remedy a contribution to the medical school, perhaps in the form of a new building dedicated to medical research, and named in her honor. Mrs. Rothweiler thought this an excellent idea, and indeed it was. The mere mention of plopping down a score or two of millions on a worthy cause had made her feel years younger already. The dean, no less pleased on his part, had proceeded to call in a slew of designers, architects, lawyers, and other such accoutrements as were necessary to so grand a project.

A rather large fly, however, had recently appeared in the ointment. After a visit to Washington, where Mrs. Rothweiler spent a lovely evening with the first lady and her president, she discovered that what the country needed was not more electron microscopes, but more primary care doctors. Mrs. Rothweiler was not exactly sure what a primary care doctor was, relying, as she did, on the practitioners of Boston, Rochester, and Houston for her medical needs. She had a vague notion that they had to do with taking care of *the people,* and as such she thought them an excellent addition to her charitable portfolio, on a par with the hospital she had commissioned in Nigeria and the woolen factory she had acquired to provide mittens for the homeless.

When she told Dean Cabot Cabot of her new interest, he agreed wholeheartedly. The dean was a flexible man when it came to benefaction. He was not one to look a gift horse in the mouth. At the time of my call to him, Dean Cabot Cabot had eagerly mounted his new steed. He was, however, was still uncertain as to which direction it would take him. On the day of our appointed visit, the question was very much on his mind.

The dean arrived a few minutes early. He wanted, he explained, to take a look at the hospital before we had our chat. He thought it would be *instructive*. Since I felt considerable proprietary pride in Emmeline Talbot, I readily agreed to the request.

My office is located in the front of the hospital just to the left of the entrance lobby. From the lobby runs a long corridor that traverses the entire length of the hospital. It is the hospital's main thoroughfare. At the near end are the doctors' offices and quarters for the administration. At the other end are the hospital rooms and the nursing home. Along the way lie side doors which lead to the emergency room, the laboratory, the cafeteria, the pharmacy, and the operating room.

Several years ago the trustees decided to renovate the hospital. Although they would never admit it, the action coincided so closely to the construction of the new medical center in Hanover as to be more than coincidentally related. This latter edifice had been built in strict accordance with modern architectural principles, which decree that the appearance of a building should bear no resemblance to the function it serves. Pursuant to this, the medical center was built along the lines of an aviary, replete with high-ceilinged skylights, verdant drooping vines, and a plethora of cages full of colorful tropical birds who warbled sweetly all the day long.

Not capable of anything on such a grand scale, the trustees of Emmeline Talbot had settled for a new carpet in the corridor. A delicate shade of green interspersed with pentagonal blocks of orange and purple, it was quite a sight to behold.

As we approached the ward, we encountered a rosy cheeked woman of about sixty busily scrubbing away and humming contentedly to herself. This was Margaret Spofford. Mrs. Spofford had been the head housekeeper at Emmeline Talbot ever since it opened, and for some number of years at the old Dumster hospital before that. She looked up as we approached and greeted us with a pleasant smile.

"Good morning Margaret," I said.

Good morning, Doctor Conger," she answered in the comfortable manner of one who was happy in her work.

"I answer to Beach," I said, teasing her for her formal address.

"And I answer to Housekeeper Spofford," she replied, her eyes twinkling with cheerful good humor, "but it's not what I'm called."

"Quite a carpet you have here," said the dean, joining in. "I don't believe I've ever seen anything quite like it—In fact, I'm quite sure. Never anything like it at all."

"Nor I, sir," answered Margaret.

"You must be quite proud," he said, giving it an appreciative glance. "I'm quite envious—really I am. I'd love nothing better than to roll the whole thing up and take it back with me. But I don't suppose you'd be willing to part with it, would you?"

"Were it up to me alone, sir, I'd gladly let you. Only there's three of us in cleaning here, and without the carpet, it would leave two without a job. I'm pretty close to retirement, but the others have hopes of getting a few more years out of it still."

At the nurses station we ran into Sandra, who was just finishing her rounds. The dean, remembering her from her student days, greeted her warmly and suggested that she might want to join our tête-à-tête. He was in an expansive mood and felt that the larger the audience the better his ideas would flow. I ventured that Sandra was probably too busy with her patients to take time off on such short notice.

Not that I was disrespectful of her opinion, or even wanting to keep the dean to myself, but I will admit I was not particularly keen on the prospect of her addition to our party. I felt that my idea, like a young orchid, was in a delicate stage and might not be quite ready for exposure to the outside world.

But she was not too busy, and she readily accepted the invitation. So the three of us repaired to the cafeteria.

"The way I see it," I said, warming up to my task, "the problem is that we're taking our patients too much for granted. All these years we've treated them as a captive audience, considered that we could do with them pretty much as we would. It's not our fault, of course. The patients themselves expected it—demanded it actually. They wanted a doctor who was in charge. But today's patients are different. To them, medicine is a commodity, like cars or televisions or life insurance. They want the best deal they can get, and if they can't get it from us, they'll go to someone else."

"You're saying that we have a marketing problem, Beach," the dean interjected, "and I quite agree with you. But not just with patients. When I was in Washington, the folks in Congress were quite confrontational—almost hostile."

"That's to be expected. Remember, they may be dressed up like congressmen, or lawyers or whatever, but take off their clothes, and what do you find? Underneath it they're all patients. Every last one of them."

"Yes," he said. That may be true. But—"

"Suppose—just suppose—that when all those politicians went to their doctors, instead of sticking stuff into them and pulling stuff out of them and telling them that everything they like is bad— in short, making them feel thoroughly miserable, suppose we made them feel good—I mean, suppose we made them feel really good! What do you think they would say the next time we wanted to raise our fees to allow us a decent standard of living or asked for a few billion more for medical research?"

I related my recent experiences with Clarence Purloin and Henry Skittersly, both of whom, I am pleased to say, benefited immensely from their hospital stay, although the salutary effect on their spirits was a bit more transient than I had hoped. They both had lapsed, immediately upon being wheeled out the door and gaining sight once again of the cold cruel world, into a profound depression which had been most troublesome to shake. This minor setback, I was convinced, could be easily overcome by a longer internment and a modest increase in medication, and I was eager to try the plan again—although not, I thought, with these two. They had been given their chance, and others deserved theirs. Besides, they had made comments about the business that, while not exactly disparaging, left me with the impression that it might be somewhat difficult to get them back in the fold.

I emphasized that these cases represented only a fraction of the kinds of things that doctors could do to their patients.

"If people feel good about what we do to them, they won't complain. They will recognize what we have known all along, that when it comes to spending your money, there's no better way to do it than on a doctor."

The dean looked thoughtful, remaining silent as he awaited my further development of his opinion.

"We may not have all the answers now, but with the right research, we can find them. Research directed not toward diseases—that's what's gotten us into this pickle—but at learning more about our patients."

"We may have something here, Beach," he said brightening at the word research. "Our plan—"

"Would be to create a new branch of medical science. One that focuses on the patient. It would need its own department, and," I added with a knowing smile, "its own professors—teachers who were skilled enough in the art of medicine to assist those who know only the science."

"Bring in the best minds in the profession. Find out what makes the patient tick. What makes him happy? What makes him sad? Which tests, which operations, which drugs are most likely to increase patient satisfaction? Which should be avoided? Pleasure, not pain, would be our guiding light. Under your direction—with someone assisting who could help you to put the theories into practice—there's no limit to what we could accomplish."

"Yes," he said slowly. "I have often thought of just such a plan—although not exactly in the form you have mentioned, which has the—uh—more practical side to it."

"Are you suggesting, Beach," asked Sandra, "that instead of encouraging our patients to feel better by adopting more healthy lifestyles, we should be advocating a purely hedonistic approach?"

"Exactly! Give the customer what he wants. That's what the opposition does. You think a chiropractor hassles his patients about cholesterol? No way Jose!

"But surely you're not suggesting we abandon our current treatment strategies. That would be—"

"Not at all. But why not combine the best of both worlds? A spoonful of honey, after all, does make the medicine go down. So we mix and match. A little something to lower your blood pressure, a little something to raise your spirits. Take out a gallbladder, put in a tummy tuck. The possibilities are limitless!"

Sandra shook her head doubtfully. "I don't know, Beach. You make it sound as if patients are like sheep, and it's simply a matter of offering them a greener pasture to get them to come running. I think patients expect more than that. It may be that the best way to advance our cause is to keep doing just what we do now—only present it honest and truly—without all the hoopla."

"We've got to fight fire with fire, Sandra. It's a dog-eat-dog world out there."

"That may be true, Beach," she said quietly, "but we're not veterinarians."

Chapter 28

All in One Place

Sandra was paged to the emergency room.

"I really wish I could stay," she said apologizing for her abrupt departure. "Your proposal is interesting, Beach—really. I think it's a great—only" She hesitated. "Maybe a little too much. To me at least. She turned to Dean Cabot Cabot. "Nice to see you again, Dean," she said. Then she took her leave.

Although I was well prepared to rebut Sandra's arguments with plenty of my own, I will confess to being relieved that she had left. With renewed confidence in my proposition, I turned to the dean.

"The way I see it Cab, if we play our cards right, we should be able to double—quadruple, even, our share of the GNP. And not so much as a peep will you hear from those bozos in Washington."

Dean Cabot Cabot looked puzzled. "But who would pay for it?" he asked.

"Patients."

"Patients?"

"Yup. They'll pay, all right—and willingly, too. Look at what they spend now on stuff like alcohol, electronic gadgets, cosmetics, vacations. We can get it all. All we have to do is convince the average Joe that we can do more to make him feel good him than a day at the beach, and we are in the clover."

"That's a pretty tall order, Beach. Patients are creatures of habit after all."

"Sure they are, but who is better qualified to change those habits than we are? And who is better qualified to develop the tools to change them than you!"

"There is something in what you say, Beach," he nodded slowly. "Still, there is a certain something of this that smacks of the, uh— too *much*—wouldn't you agree?"

"We can't be sticks-in-the-mud, Cab. This is no time for second thoughts. This is a time for action."

"Perhaps—" he said looking thoughtful. "Perhaps. Well, all this has been most interesting, Beach. Most interesting indeed. You have certainly given me food for thought—more than I can digest at one sitting. But it was a substantial meal—and it may be just what the doctor ordered. I'll be in touch. You haven't heard the last from me. Depend upon it."

Two weeks later he called. He had been quite "preoccupied" with our discussion, he said, and had come to the conclusion that the medical school did need a fresh approach to things. With the help of a generous donation, he was going to create an entirely new department, the Olivia Rothweiler Department of Patientology. The trustees of the Medical School had given the plan full approval, and he was hoping to name someone to head it up within the month.

"As someone who has assisted me immeasurably in my development of this concept," he said, "I would like you to come on board our planning team."

The dean explained that it was someone like me—someone *very much* like me, he emphasized, whom he was looking for to head the department. He knew I was very busy with my practice, and it was a terrible imposition, but if I could possibly—In short, he pleaded so desperately for my help, that even had I not a minute to spare, I could hardly have refused him.

The dean didn't come right out and say it, but the implication was clear. The job was mine for the asking.

With visions of a future free of my festering practice, free of the demanding patients, and free of the shadow of Sandra, I told Dean Cabot Cabot he could count me in.

It was some groundwork. Each new issue spawned a committee, and each new committee a report, and one month turned into two, and the two into three, and by the end of four months we seemed no closer to completion than when we had started.

Six months later Sandra came into my office. She was uncharacteristically glum.

"Got a minute?" she asked. "I need someone to talk to."

Nuisance or no, I was fond of Sandra. Were it not for her effect on my practice, I would have enjoyed our partnership wholeheartedly. Her open, honest nature was a source of comfort, and on more than a few occasions, I had, within bounds, unburdened myself to her. I was glad to return the favor.

"I feel terrible," she said disconsolately. "Absolutely awful. Something has come up. Something I never expected. Something that—that—I'm going to have to leave Dumster!" She blurted out, bursting into tears.

While such an announcement might have been met with bearable regret a few months ago, now, on the eve of my appointment, it was a cause of genuine discomfort. I couldn't imagine what kind of a fix she had gotten into. Certainly it was nothing professional. On the personal side—well there was nothing I knew about, but Sandra kept pretty much to herself, and in a small town, wickets can sometimes get pretty sticky.

I tried to persuade her that whatever it was, it would pass in time, for she really was, I declared, quite beloved by all.

"Oh I know that," she said still sobbing. "That's not the problem. That's not it at all."

"What is it, then?"

"I've taken another job."

This *was* unexpected news! Sandra had seemed very happy in Dumster, and although the pay was not up with more prosperous areas, a doctor here still could make a very decent living. True she had student loans to pay off, but those had never seemed to trouble her. There was her mother in Indiana. She was badly crippled with arthritis, and Sandra's father had died unexpectedly not too long ago leaving her without help and in some financial straits. Yes, I thought on futher consideration, Sandra might well have grounds for seeking a more remunerative practice.

"I would hate to see you leave," I said. "And I would do my best to convince you otherwise, but I know you better than to think you would make a decision like this without careful consideration and on any other than the highest principles. If you seek better opportunities, I am sure it is with the best of reasons."

Sandra shook her head. "It's not about money."

"What is it then?"

"Dean Cabot Cabot has offered me a job! It's in the new department he's setting up. Oh, Beach, ever since I can remember, I've wanted to be a teacher. I think it's in my blood. My mother was a teacher. My father was a teacher. And my three brothers are teachers. But I hate to leave my patients. And I hate to leave you— you've done so much for me. I feel as if I'm deserting you."

"If that's your only fear, Sandra then you may rest easy. In fact, I couldn't be happier. For I also expect to be part of the department, although in a slightly different capacity."

"That's super!" she said brightening. "If I had only known that you were—but it's funny the dean didn't say anything about it to me."

"I think he wants to keep everything hush-hush until the formal announcement."

"You mean tomorrow."

"Tomorrow?"

"Yes. Right here at Emmeline Talbot. He told me he thought it would be only fitting."

This was all a little peculiar. I could understand the dean wanting to surprise me with the news of my appointment. He was like that. But why then did he tell Sandra?

"Er—What else did he say about the plans?" I asked cautiously.

"It's going to be a big whoop-de-do, with the press, and all the trustees—even Senator Leahy and the governor will be there. If you want to know the truth, I'm a little nervous."

"That's only natural. Still, it shouldn't be too bad. After all, the instructors aren't likely to be the main source of attention."

"That's just it. There won't be any others. Tomorrow is just for the chair of the department."

"Just the chair."

"I asked him to include everybody—I really don't like being the center of attention—but there was no talking him out of it. He wanted it for the chair and no one else."

"No one else."

"It just doesn't seem possible, does it? I mean, here I am, only one year in practice, and now I'm to be a professor. I really don't feel I deserve it. There are others with so much more experience than I—you for example." She paused. "But I don't guess anyone could drag you away from here, no matter what they offered."

"No, I don't suppose anyone could."

"You're so committed to your patients—to Dumster. You'll be here forever I guess. You know, in a way I'm envious. This town, this hospital, these people—it's your home. And mine—"

Sandra looked at me wistfully for a minute. Then, collecting herself, she gave a small sigh, shook her shoulders, and smiled.

"Well, I feel a lot better about it now. You've perked me up ever so much, Beach. I can't thank you enough, really I can't."

She grasped both my hands and squeezed them tightly. Then she gave me a big hug and bounced out of the room, leaving alone with his thoughts, kindly old Doc Conger of Dumster.

Epilogue

The day after the announcement of Sandra's appointment I was in Contremond's stocking up on a hefty supply of Heath Bar Crunch and Chunky Monkey. I've found this to be an antidepressant one-two that can lick Prozac any day of the week. I chanced upon Fusswood, who was embarked upon a similar mission.

We fell to talking about Sandra.

"At first it hit me like a lead balloon, Doc," he said. "She is one helluva doctor, and I'm going to miss her. I don't know when I've ever felt so good about myself as when I'd just seen her. She had that way about her. You know what I mean?"

"Yes," I said. "I know what you mean."

"Still, I can hardly complain. She's going on to greater things, and if she winds up teaching half of what she knows to other doctors, we might all be better off. Lord knows you guys sure could use a dose of the Smarts."

"Oh?"

"I don't mean you, Doc. I mean, you're a pretty good guy. A little old fashioned maybe, but still—you're all right."

"Thank you Fusswood," I said dryly, "for the compliment."

"Don't get bent out of shape, Doc. I'm only kidding. Anyway, it looks like we're stuck with each other again. I suppose it's only right. She was just *too* good. But you—well, I guess we all get what we deserve. Not that I'm complaining, mind you." He gave me a friendly clap on the back. "I mean, hey, we're Dumster, you and I. Dumster all the way."

Difficult as it was to construe this remark as a compliment, Fusswood had pointed out something I had not considered. There was another side to this whole affair.

"You are right, Fusswood," I said returning the salute with an arm around his shoulder. "We *do* deserve each other. And speaking of which, it might be wise for you to make an appointment. Just to get *reacquainted*, as it were."

Fusswood nodded. "Sounds like a good idea, Doc. But remember, it's not like it used to be. You're dealing with a different Fusswood now."

"A brand new model."

"No jerking me around with any unnecessary tests."

"Perish the thought."

"No experimenting with fancy new drugs."

"Heaven forbid!"

"No cover ups. Only the straight stuff from now on."

"You took the words right out of my mouth."

"Partners in this. Both of us equals."

"Your wish is my command."

"In that case, Doc," he grinned sticking out his hand, "you got a deal. I'll call Maggie this afternoon. You'll see, it'll be better for both of us."

"I couldn't agree more."

Fusswood turned to go.

"Oh by the way, Fusswood—" I said catching him by the arm.

"Yes, Doc?"

"There is one thing I'd like to discuss with you before we get too far down the road."

"Sure thing, Doc. Discuss away."

"About that cholesterol of yours—"